Applied Physics Experiments

Applied Physics

EXPERIMENTS

Dr. Sushil Kumar Jain
M.Sc. (Physics), Ph.D., (Solid State Physics)

Senior Lecturer
(Department of Physics)
Amity Institute of Applied Sciences
Amity School of Engineering & Technology
Amity University, Jaipur (Rajasthan)

Dr. Manjeet Singh
M.Sc. (Physics), Ph.D. (Nonlinear Optics)

Lecturer
(Department of Physics)
Amity Institute of Applied Sciences
Amity School of Engineering & Technology
Amity University, Noida (U.P.)

AN ISO 9001:2008 CERTIFIED COMPANY
VAYU EDUCATION OF INDIA
2/25, Ansari Road, Darya Ganj, New Delhi-110 002

Applied Physics Experiments

ISBN: 978-93-80712-67-3

First Edition: 2010

Price: ₹100.00

Printed & bound in India

Published by:

AN ISO 9001:2008 CERTIFIED COMPANY

VAYU EDUCATION OF INDIA

2/25, Ansari Road, Darya Ganj, New Delhi-110 002

Ph.: 91-11-47236600, 41564445

Fax: 91-11-41564440

E-mail: vei@veiindia.com

Web: www.veiindia.com

Dedicated

to

Our

Parents

Preface

This book is written keeping in mind the requirements of B. Tech. students of various Engineering and Technical courses. Most of the experiments included in the book from the syllabus of Amity University, Noida and Lucknow Campuses (Uttar Pradesh), Amity University, Jaipur (Rajasthan), Amity University, Manesar (Haryana) and other Technical Universities of India.

Following are the salient features of the book:

- According to the latest system of examination adopted by most of the Indian universities, the candidates are required to write the theory of the experiment before starting the experimental work. With this aim in view a brief and relevant theoretical discussion of the experiment has been included in the body of the experiment proper, so that a student actually reads and understands it before starting the work.
- A brief discussion of the apparatus required during the experiment has been given and the range of various measuring instruments has been specified so that the observations can be taken with a fair degree of accuracy.
- The procedure has been divided into steps so that a student may be able to proceed systematically even without the direct guidance of a teacher.
- The system of recording the observations in a tabular form has been encouraged throughout the text so that various readings can be compared at a glance.
- The precautions have not only been given at the end of the experiment but also have been included in the instructions so that a student actually observes them even when he is performing the experiment.
- As there is a growing tendency on the part of examiners to ask oral questions about the experiments done by a student in the examination, a number of such questions with answers have been given at the end of each experiment.

It is hoped that with all these and other features this book will prove very useful for the students.

Authors

Acknowledgement

We are thankful to Dr. Ashok K. Chauhan, Founder President, Amity University (RBEF), Mr. Atul Chauhan, Chancellor, Amity University, Noida, Mr. Aseem K. Chauhan, Chancellor, Amity University Rajasthan, Jaipur, Maj. Gen. K. Jai Singh, Vice Chancellor, Amity University, Noida and Prof. Raj Singh, Vice Chancellor, Amity University Jaipur, Rajasthan, for their inspiration.

Our sincere thanks are due to Prof. Dr. Balvinder Shukla, Pro Vice Chancellor (Academic) and Director General, ASET, Noida and Prof. (Dr.) Om Vir Singh, Director, Amity School of Engineering for his valuable suggestions and comments. We are also thankful to our colleagues from Department of Physics, Amity University for their cooperation during preparation of the manuscript.

I (Dr. S.K. Jain) can very well feel and the love of my wife Dr. Reena Jain and my son Chinmay Jain who have always been my aspirations.

I (Dr. M. Singh) can very well feel and the love of my wife Mrs. Anita Devi & my nephew Parveen who have always been my aspirations.

Any suggestions towards further improvement will be thankfully acknowledged and incorporated in the next edition.

The unfailing efforts of publishers, VAYU Education of India, in getting this book published well in time, deserve high praise.

Authors

APPLIED PHYSICS EXPERIMENTS

For B. Tech., First Year Students
of

Amity University, Noida and Lucknow Campuses
(Uttar Pradesh)

•

Amity University Jaipur
(Rajasthan)

•

Amity University, Manesar
(Haryana)
&
Other Technical Universities of India

Syllabus

APPLIED PHYSICS EXPERIMENTS

1. To determine the wavelength of sodium light by Newton's rings appartatus.
2. To determine the dispersive power of the material of prism with the help of spectrometer.
3. To determine the specific rotation of sugar solution by Bi-quartz or Laurent half shade polarimeter.
4. To determine the speed of ultrasonic waves in a liquid by diffraction method.
5. To determine the width of a narrow slit using diode laser by diffraction phenomena.
6. To determine the temperature coefficient of resistance for platinum using a Platinum resistance thermometer and a Callender and Griffith bridge.
7. To determine the value of specific charge (e/m) of an electron by Thomson's method.
8. To determine the internal resistance of Leclenche cell with the help of potentiometer.
9. To determine the resistance per unit length of a Carey Foster's bridge wire and also to find out the specific resistance of a given wire.
10. To plot graph showing the variation of magnetic field with distance along the axis of a circular coil carrying current and hence estimate the radius of the coil.
11. To determine the value of acceleration due to gravity in the laboratory using bar pendulum.
12. To determine the moment of inertia of a flywheel about its own axis of rotation.
13. To determine the density of the material of a given wire with the help of a sonometer.
14. To determine the wavelength of prominent spectral lines of mercury by plane diffraction grating in first and second order spectrum.
15. To determine the thickness of the given wire using wedge method.
16. To determine the wavelength of He-Ne Laser light using single slit.
17. To determine the frequency of an electrically maintained tunning fork by Melde's method.
18. To study the variation of magnetic field along the axis of Helmholtz coil and to find the reduction factor.
19. To draw the V-I Characteristics of a forward and reverse biased PN-junction diode.
20. To determine the frequency of A.C. mains by an electromagnet by using a sonometer.
21. To determine the band gap of Ge-Crystal by four probe method.
22. To draw VI characteristics of a photocell and to verify the inverse square law of radiation.
23. To determine the acceleration due to gravity (g) by Kater's reversible pendulum.
24. To study the characteristics of photovoltaic (Solar cell).

Contents

MEASURING INSTRUMENTS

Several measuring devices and techniques are standard tools of mechanics. They will be introduced here so that a student will understand them well enough to use them when the need arises in this course.

1. VERNIER CALIPERS

Vernier calipers consist of a rectangular steel bar graduated in centimeters, as shown in Fig. 1. This is known as main scale. Over this scale slides a small scale called the vernier scale.

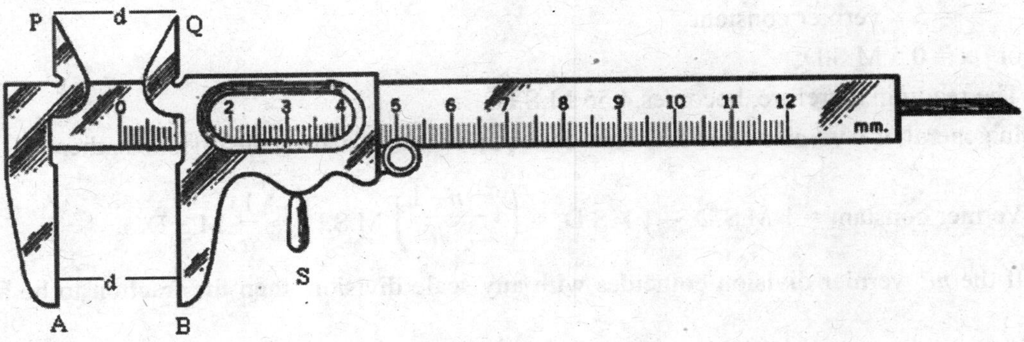

Fig. 1 Vernier caliper

The instrument has got two jaws, A and B. The jaw A is fixed at the end of the rectangular bar on the zero side, while the other jaw B is movable and can slide along the main scale. Each jaw is at right angles to the main scale and the movable jaw can be fixed at any position by the screw S. The two vernier scales are attached to the movable jaw as shown. Usually when the two jaws are touching each other, the zero of the vernier scale coincides with zero of the main scale.

In some forms of the instrument the jaws project in the upper part as shown at P and Q. These projecting jaws are used to measure the internal diameters of the tubes. The movable jaw also carries a thin rectangular rod which is used to measure the depth of vessels.

Vernier constant: To understand how the fractions of the smallest scale division is read accurately with the help of a vernier; consider a vernier scale having 10 equal divisions.

Let these 10 vernier divisions coincide with 9 main scale divisions. Since 10 divisions of the vernier scale coincide with 9 main scale divisions, therefore

$$1 \text{ V.S.D.} = \frac{9}{10} \text{M.S.D.}$$

or $$1 \text{ M.S.D.} - 1 \text{ V.S.D.} = \frac{1}{10} \text{M.S.D.} = 0.1 \text{ M.S.D.}$$

The difference between one main scale division and one vernier scale division is called the vernier constant or the least count of the vernier.

Now consider that the zero of the vernier lies between 4.5 and 4.6 as shown in Fig. 1.2.

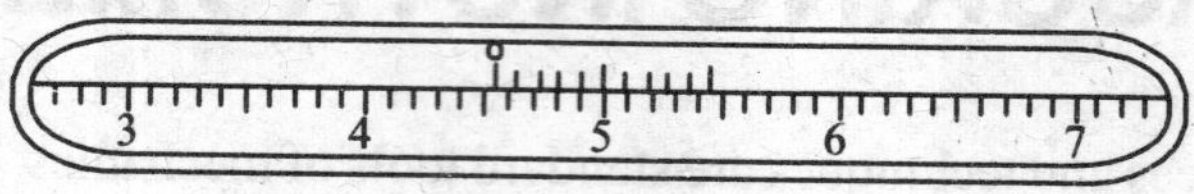

Fig. 2 Measurement using vernier callipers

It is clear from the figure that the 5th vernier division coincides with a main scale division. If we denote the fraction after 4.5 by x, then

4.5 + x + 5 V.S.D. = 4.5 + 5 V.S.D

or x = 5 M.S.D. – 5 V.S.D. = 5 (1 M.S.D. – 1 V.S.D.)

= 5 × vernier constant

or x = 0.5 M.S.D.

The reading, therefore, becomes 4.55 M.S.D.

In general, if n vernier scale divisions are equal to (n - 1) main scale divisions, then

$$\text{Vernier constant} = 1\text{ M.S.D.} - 1\text{ V.S.D.} = \left(1 - \frac{n-1}{n}\right)\text{ M.S.D.} = \frac{1}{n}\text{ M.S.D.}$$

If the mth vernier division coincides with any scale division, then the fraction to be added $= m \times \frac{1}{n}$

Hence the rule to read the fraction of a scale division is to multiply the number of the vernier division which coincides with any scale division with the vernier constant.

Rule to find the vernier constant:

(i) Find the magnitude of the smallest division on the main scale.

(ii) Count the total number of divisions on the vernier scale.

(iii) Slide the movable jaw so that the zero mark (the first division) of the vernier scale coincides with any of the main scale divisions.

(iv) Find the number of main scale divisions, which coincide with the total number of vernier scale divisions. Calculate the vernier constant as explained above.

Many instruments which are used for measurement are provided with vernier arrangement. Some of these are discussed below:

Linear vernier

(i) **Fortin's barometer:** The Fortin's barometer (Fig. 3) is used to find the value of atmospheric pressure. It is a variation of the classic Torricelli barometer working on the same principles as any other barometer but with a different construction. The one most notable difference between the two is that the Fortin barometer has the cistern made out of leather instead of metal like the aforementioned mercury barometer. The way the Fortin barometer works is different in a sense that it uses atmospheric pressure to balance the weight of a column of mercury against it. From that, any change in the atmospheric pressure is accompanied by an immediate change in the level of the mercury and can be measured against the scale engraved on the barometer. To be able to use the Fortin barometer in good measuring conditions we should aim for exposure spots where the temperature is uniform, the light is good and the Fortin barometer has a solid mounting both vertically and horizontally.

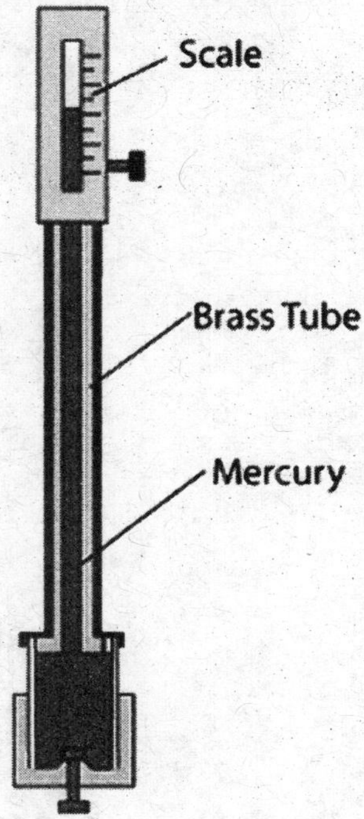

Fig. 3 Fortin's barometer

In this case, let 10 V.S.D. coincide with 19 M.S.D. and 1 M.S.D. is 1 millimeter. To find vernier constant each V.S.D. is supposed to be further divided into two, thereby making a total of 20 such divisions. The vernier constant of this new vernier scale ill be as follows:

20 supposed V.S.D. = 19 M.S.D.

$$1 \text{ supposed V.S.D.} = \frac{19}{20} \text{ M.S.D.}$$

$$\text{Vernier constant} = 1 \text{ M.S.D.} - 1 \text{ V.S.D.} = \left(1-\frac{19}{20}\right) \text{M.S.D.} = \frac{1}{20} \text{ mm} = 0.05 \text{ mm.}$$

In fact each vernier division is twice this supposed division.

Therefore, Vernier constant = 2 × 0.05 = 0.1 mm = 0.01 cm.

In second step of this type instrument 20 V.S.D. coincide with 19 M.S.D. and 1 M.S.D. is 1 mm. The vernier constant of such kind of Fortin's barometer will be as follows:

20 V.S.D. = 19 M.S.D.

$$1 \text{ V.S.D.} = \frac{19}{20} \text{ M.S.D.}$$

$$\text{Vernier constant} = 1 \text{ M.S.D.} - 1 \text{ V.S.D.} = \left(1-\frac{19}{20}\right) \text{M.S.D.} = \frac{1}{20} \text{ mm} = 0.05 \text{ mm} = 0.005 \text{ cm.}$$

(ii) Travelling microscope: A travelling microscope (Fig. 4) is an instrument for measuring length with a resolution of about 0.05 - 0.1 mm. It is composed of a microscope mounted on two rails fixed to a supporting structure. The position of the microscope can be varied coarsely by sliding along the rails, or finely by turning a screw. Position of the microscope is read by a vernier. Purpose of the microscope is to aim at reference marks with much higher accuracy compared with bare eyes. It is used in labs to measure refractive index of liquids using the geometrical concepts of ray optics. It is also used to measure very short distances like diameter of capillary tubes with precision and diameter of Newton's rings in interference experiments.

Fig. 4 Travelling microscope

In this case, let 25 V.S.D. coincide with 25 M.S.D. and each scale division is 0.5 mm.

Therefore, 25 V.S.D. = 24 M.S.D.

or 1 V.S.D. = $\frac{24}{25}$ M.S.D.

Therefore, Vernier constant = 1 M.S.D. – 1 V.S.D. = $\left(1-\frac{24}{25}\right)$ M.S.D. = $\frac{1}{25}$ M.S.D.

= $\frac{1}{25}\times 0.5$ mm = 0.002 cm.

Circular vernier

(i) Spectrometer: A spectrometer (Fig. 5) is an instrument used to produce spectrum of a light source. The parts of a basic spectrometer are: a collimator, a telescope, and a prism table. The collimator has an arrangement of lenses. A slit of adjustable width is provided on the head of collimator. A light source illuminating the slit that acts as an object for lenses. The optical instrument is mounted on the prism table. The telescope is used to view the spectrum. The rotation of telescope can be read on two vernier scales provided on the base of prism table.

Fig. 5 Spectrometer

In this case let 30 V.S.D. coincide with 29 M.S.D. and magnitude of each scale division is 0.5 degree.

Therefore, 30 V.S.D. = 29 M.S.D.

$$\text{or } 1 \text{ V.S.D.} = \frac{29}{30} \text{ M.S.D.}$$

$$\text{Therefore, Vernier constant} = 1 \text{ M.S.D.} - 1 \text{ V.S.D.} = \left(1-\frac{29}{30}\right) \text{ M.S.D.} = \frac{1}{30} \text{ M.S.D.} = \frac{1}{30}\times 0.5 \text{ Degree} = \frac{1}{60} \text{ Degree} = 1 \text{ minute.}$$

(ii) Sextant: A sextant (Fig. 6) is an instrument used to measure the angle between any two visible objects. Its primary use is to determine the angle between a celestial object and the horizon which is known as the altitude. Making this measurement is known as sighting the object, shooting the object, or taking a sight. The angle, and the time when it was measured, can be used to calculate a position line on a nautical or aeronautical chart. A common use of the sextant is to sight the sun at noon to find one's latitude. Since the sextant can be used to measure the angle between any two objects, it can be held horizontally to measure the angle between any two landmarks which will allow for calculation of a position on a chart. A sextant can also be used to measure the Lunar distance between the moon and another celestial object (e.g., star, planet) in order to determine Greenwich time. The scale of a sextant has a length of 1/6 of a full circle (60°); hence the sextant's name.

Fig. 6 Sextant

In this case usually 60 V.S.D. coincide with 119 M.S.D. and each scale division is equal to 10 minutes. To find the vernier constant each vernier division is supposed to be further divided into two thereby making a total of 120 such vernier divisions. The vernier constant of this new vernier will be as follows:

120 V.S.D. = 119 M.S.D.

or 1 V.S.D. = $\frac{119}{120}$ M.S.D.

Therefore, Vernier constant = 1 M.S.D. – 1 V.S.D. = $\left(1-\frac{119}{120}\right)$ M.S,D. = $\frac{1}{120}$ M.S.D. = $\frac{1}{120}\times 10$ minute = 2 seconds.

In fact each vernier division is twice this value.

(iii) Polarimeter: A polarimeter (Fig. 7) is a scientific instrument used to measure the angle of rotation caused by passing polarized light through an optically active substance.

Fig. 7 Polarimeter

In this case each division on the circular scale of the polarimeter is 1 degree and 10 V.S.D. coincide with 9 M.S.D. Therefore

10 V.S.D. = 9 M.S.D.

$$\text{or } 1 \text{ V.S.D.} = \frac{9}{10} \text{ M.S.D.}$$

$$\text{Therefore, Vernier constant} = 1 \text{ M.S.D.} - 1 \text{ V.S.D.} = \left(1-\frac{9}{10}\right) \text{M.S.D.} = \frac{1}{10} \text{ M.S.D.}$$

$$= \frac{1}{10} \times 60' = 6'$$

2. SCREW GAUGE

It is based upon the principle of a screw and consists of a U-shaped frame as shown in Fig. 8. The object to be measured is placed between the fixed jaw (A) and the movable jaw (R) and the jaw is gently closed on the object. The movable jaw (R) of the screw gauge is driven by a precise and uniform screw. A typical metric instrument has the main scale marked to 0.5 mm. The circumference of the rotating handle (circular scale, T) is subdivided into 50 or 100 equal subdivisions. One rotation of the handle carries the screw a distance of 0.5 mm along the main scale (S). Therefore the markings on the circular scale allow one to read hundredths of millimeters.

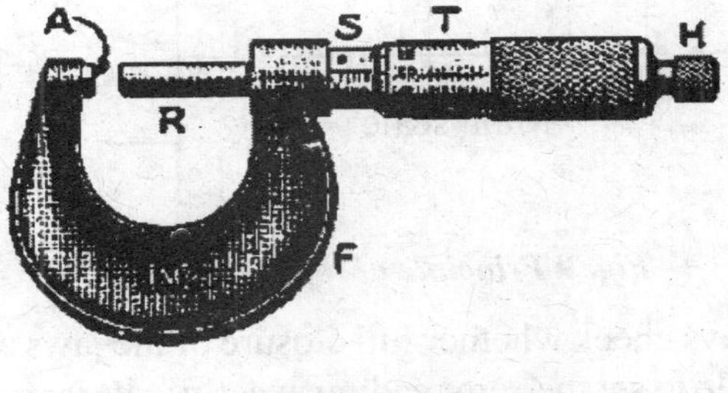

Fig. 8 Screw gauge

Least count: The least count of the screw gauge is defined as the distance through which the screw moves backward or forward when the cap is rotated through one division on the circular scale.

Rule to find the least count: To find the last count of a screw gauge, we first determine the pitch.

Pitch of a screw is defined as the distance between two consecutive threads taken parallel to its axis and is measured by the distance through which the screw moves forward or backward when one complete rotation is given to the circular cap.

Rule to find the pitch:

(i) Rotate the circular scale T and coincide the zero mark with the reference line. Note the reading of the pitch scale.

(ii) Give four complete rotations to the circular scale and again note the reading on the pitch scale.
(iii) Calculate the pitch by the formula:

$$\text{Pitch} = \frac{\text{Distance traveled on the pitch scale}}{\text{Number of rotations}}$$

To find the least count, note the number of divisions on the circular scale. Then

$$\text{Least count} = \frac{\text{Pitch of the screw}}{\text{Number of divisions on the circular scale}}$$

In Fig. 9 the reading on the main scale is more than 5.5 mm but less than 5.6 mm. The circular scale reading is 27.5, so the instrument's length reading is 5.5 + 0.275 = 5.775 mm. We must sure whether the reading lies in the lower or upper half of a millimeter. If it is in the upper half, be sure to include the extra half millimeter in the final value. On most screw gauges, the half-mm marks are on the opposite side of the line from the mm marks. This makes the scale easier to read.
Special care must be exercised when using this instrument. Close the jaws on an object, then tighten the jaws using the slip clutch (H) only. This ensures sufficiently snug closure, but prevents the jaws being closed so forcefully that the instrument might be bent, and the jaws thrown out of alignment.

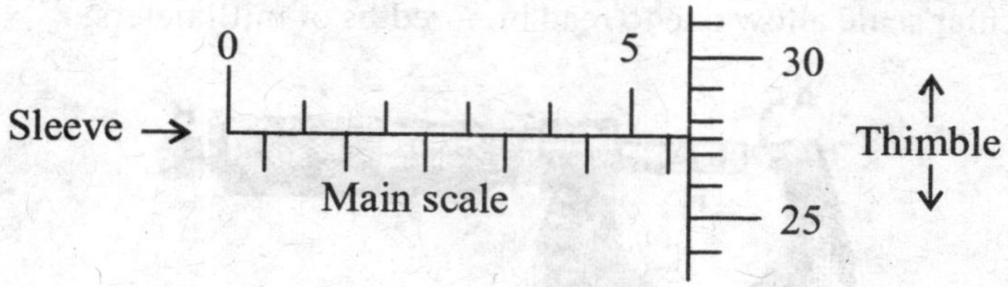

Fig. 9 Principle of the screw gauge

Zero correction: Always check whether full closure of the jaws actually gives a zero reading. Special wrenches are available to set the zero reading exactly. Alternatively, the zero reading may be treated as a correction value to be added to (or subtracted from) all readings made with the instrument. This value is called a "zero correction.".

3. SPHEROMETER

A spherometer is an instrument used for measuring very small distances. It also works on the principle of a micrometer screw. It is generally used for measuring the thickness of a thin plate and for determining the radius of curvature of spherical surfaces such as lenses or mirrors.

It consists of a metal framework supported on three fixed legs of equal length. The end of the three legs lies at the corners of an equilateral triangle. An accurately cur screw works through a threaded hole at the centre of the framework. The screw terminates at the top into a milled head and carries a large graduated disc as shown in Fig. 10.

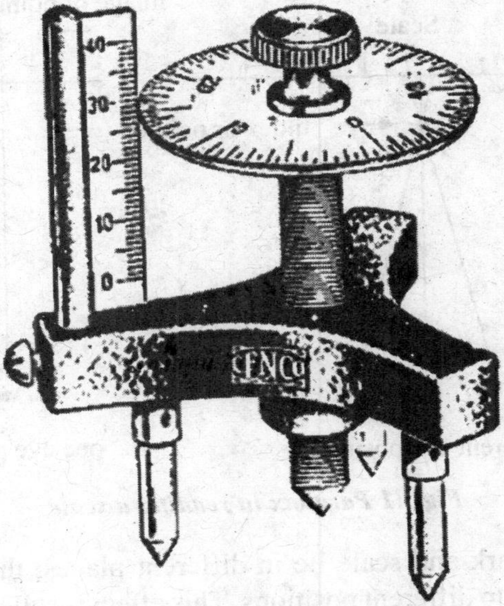

Fig. 10 A spherometer

The lower end of this screw forms the central leg of the instrument. A small vertical scale marked on millimeters or half millimeters is fixed at one end of the frame with its graduations close to those on the circular disc. The end of the circular disc is divided into a large number of equal divisions, generally 50 or 100.

Least count: The least count of a spherometer is the smallest distance that can be measured with it. It is the distance moved by the screw when it is turned through one division on the circular scale.

Rule to find the least count:

(i) Bring the zero of the circular scale against a division mark on the mm scale.

(ii) Give four complete rotations to the screw and find the distance moved by it on the millimeter scale.

(iii) Divide this distance by 4 to get the pitch of the screw.

(iv) Divide the pitch by the total number of divisions on the circular scale to get the least count of the spherometer.

A spherometer is used to find the radius of curvature of curved surfaces.

4. PARALLAX

Whenever a pointer or index mark must be read against a scale, it is best to have the two in exactly the same plane. Good quality instruments are designed to ensure this. But in some cases this is not possible, as with the movable needle on a voltmeter or ammeter. The needle must be slightly above the calibrated scale, to avoid the needle touching the scale. The marks around the circular scale of a micrometer caliper can not touch the scale on the main shaft, for the same reason.

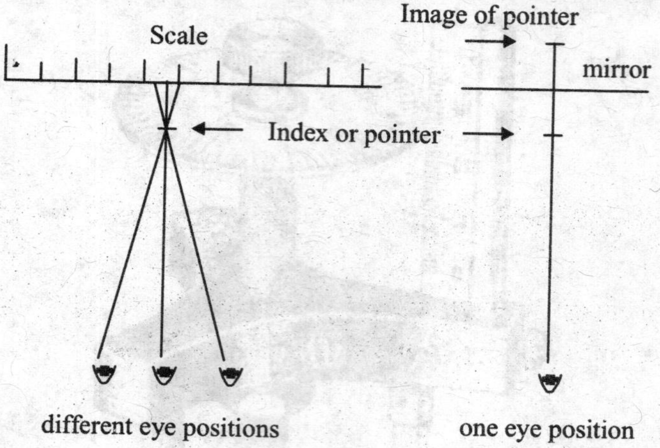

Fig. 11 Parallax in reading a scale

Whenever the index mark and scale lie in different planes, the "reading" we observe can change as we move your head to different positions. This effect is called "parallax." To eliminate its effect on measurements, be certain that our line of sight is exactly perpendicular to the scale.

Some electrical meters have a mirror beneath the scale so that we can first line up our eye so that the pointer and its image seem to coincide. This ensures that our line of sight is perpendicular to the scale.

SOURCES OF LIGHT

We shall discuss here some sources of light which are frequently used in this course.

1. BUNSEN'S FLAME

It is the simplest method of producing spectrum of various inorganic substances e.g. sodium, potassium, lithium, calcium, barium, strontium etc. A brush of asbestos is impregnated with a solution of the salt and then held in the frame. Owing to the high temperature the salt volatizes and gives the spectrum of the metal.

2. DISCHARGE TUBE

It consists of a glass tube having two aluminium electrodes sealed at the two ends as shown in Fig. 1. The tube is filled with a gas at a pressure ranging between 5 and 10 mm of mercury. When connected to the secondary of an induction coil or a high voltage transformer a discharge passes and the gas gives its characteristic spectrum. The colour of discharge depends upon the nature of the gas, being red for neon, pink for helium and so on.

3. SODIUM VAPOUR LAMP

A sodium vapour lamp is a gas discharge lamp which uses sodium in an excited state to produce light. It consists of a discharge tube made from a heat resistant glass, containing a small amount of metallic sodium, neon gas and two electrodes, as shown in Fig. 1. Neon gas is added to start the discharge and to develop enough heat to vaporize the sodium. Because of low pressure inside the tube, a sufficiently long tube required to obtain more light. To reduce the overall dimension of the lamp, this tube is generally bent into U-shape.

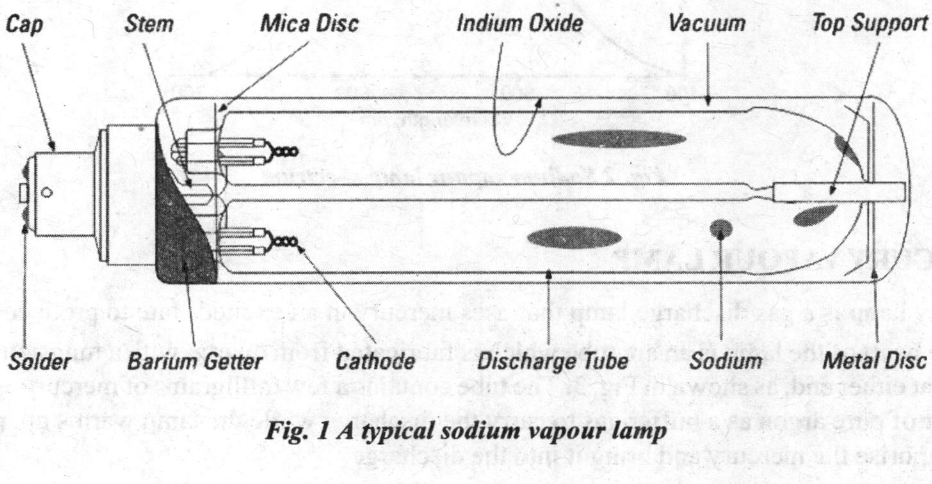

Fig. 1 A typical sodium vapour lamp

The light produced by this lamp is yellowish which is produced at its optimum pressure of about 0.004 mm of mercury. This pressure is obtained at a temperature of about 280° C and so it becomes necessary to maintain this temperature. For this purpose the discharge tube is enclosed in a double walled flask to prevent lose of heat. The double walled flask is interchangeable and can be fitted on to another tube. While replacing the inner tube we must be very careful because if it is broken and sodium comes in contact with moisture, it may result in fire.

All electric discharge lamps require a higher voltage at the time of starting and low voltage during operation. Generally, sodium vapour lamps are operated by a high leakage reactance transformer. At starting a high voltage of about 450 volts is applied across the lamp which is sufficient to start the discharge. When the lamp is fully operative after 10-15 minutes, the voltage across it falls to about 150 volts. Because of the high reactance of circuit, the power factor is low and hence a p.f improvement capacitor is connected.

The efficiency of a low pressure sodium vapour lamp is very high (about 40 - 50 lumens/watt) and it produces a light of particular wavelength having yellow color. Sodium lamps are mainly employed for street, high way and airfield lighting where color distinction is not so necessary.

The spectral response of sodium vapour lamp is shown in Fig. 2.

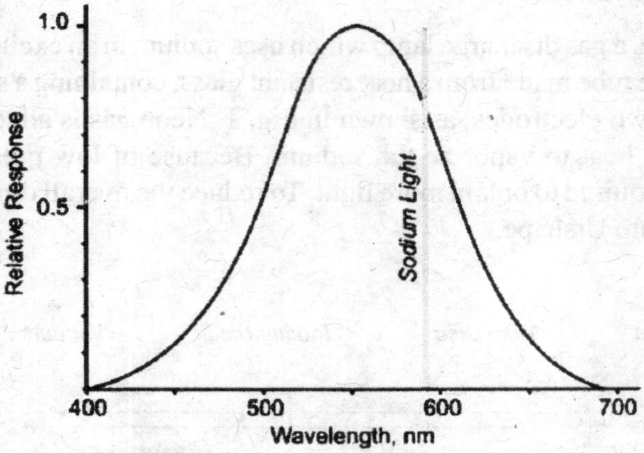

Fig. 2 Sodium vapour lamp spectrum

4. MERCURY VAPOUR LAMP

A mercury lamp is a gas discharge lamp that uses mercury in an excited state to produce light.

The heart of the lamp is an arc tube which is fabricated from quartz, with a tungsten electrode disposed at either end, as shown in Fig. 3. The tube contains a few milligrams of mercury and around 25-50 torr of pure argon as a buffer gas to carry the discharge while the lamp warms up, producing heat to vaporise the mercury and bring it into the discharge.

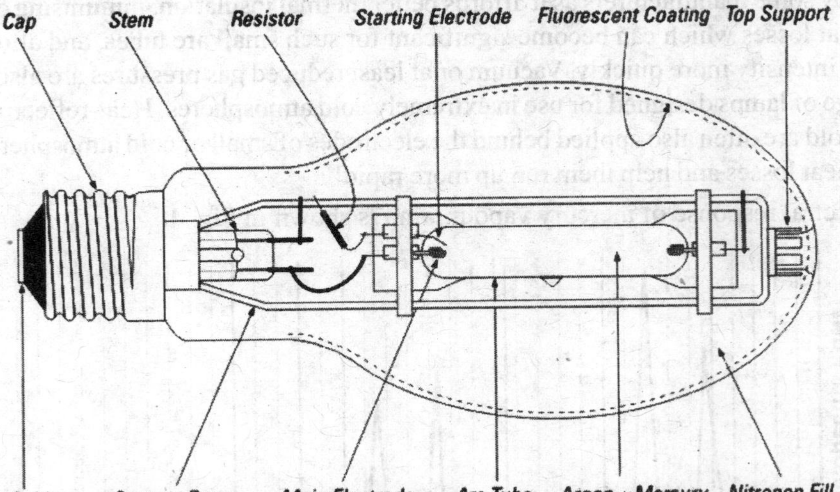

Fig. 3 A typical mercury lamp

An auxiliary starting electrode is placed next to one of the main electrodes to facilitate lamp ignition. When the lamp is first energised the full open circuit voltage is applied across the arc tube. The distance between the electrodes is so large that the resulting voltage gradient is not high enough to cause ionisation of the gas filling. However the same voltage is also applied between one electrode and the auxiliary via a small resistor. The gap between these electrodes is much smaller, and the voltage gradient is sufficiently high that ionisation will occur. A small discharge strikes, the series resistor of 10-30 kW limiting the current flow to about one thousandth of the normal lamp current. Once free electrons, ions and photons have been produced in the arc tube it is then very easy to strike a discharge across the main electrodes. The discharge quickly makes this transition because it can then bypass the starting resistor, and there is no electrical resistance between the main electrodes. Some lamps, particularly high wattage types often include two auxiliary electrodes, one beside each main electrode and connected via a resistor to the opposite end of the arc tube. This is also standard practice in mercury lamps designed for use in colder atmospheres.

Once the lamp has warmed up and the mercury is fully vaporised, the discharge operates in unsaturated mercury vapour at a pressure varying from 18 bar for the smallest types, to 2 bar for the largest. The arc emits the characteristic green, yellow and violet mercury lines and there are also considerable amounts of invisible long-wave ultraviolet at 365 nm along with a broad range of shorter wavelengths. In the earliest lamps having clear outer bulbs this invisible ultraviolet radiation was completely wasted. Today the outer bulb is internally coated with a thin layer of a fluorescent phosphor which converts the ultraviolet into visible light, generally at the red end of the spectrum where the mercury output is lacking, to improve the colour rendering properties of this light source.

The outer envelope is filled with a nitrogen or argon-nitrogen mixture, or occasionally with carbon dioxide, both to prevent oxidation of the arc tube seals and to slow the rate of deterioration of certain phosphors. For low power lamps of 50 watts and below, a vacuum or argon-rich atmosphere is employed by some manufacturers as it affords better thermal insulation, minimising conducted and convected heat losses which can become significant for such small arc tubes, and allowing them to run up to full intensity more quickly. Vacuum or at least reduced gas pressures are also employed in a special range of lamps designed for use in extremely cold atmospheres. Heat-reflective coatings of platinum or gold are often also applied behind the electrodes of small or cold atmosphere lamps again to minimise heat losses and help them run up more rapidly.

The spectral response of mercury vapour lamp is shown in Fig. 4.

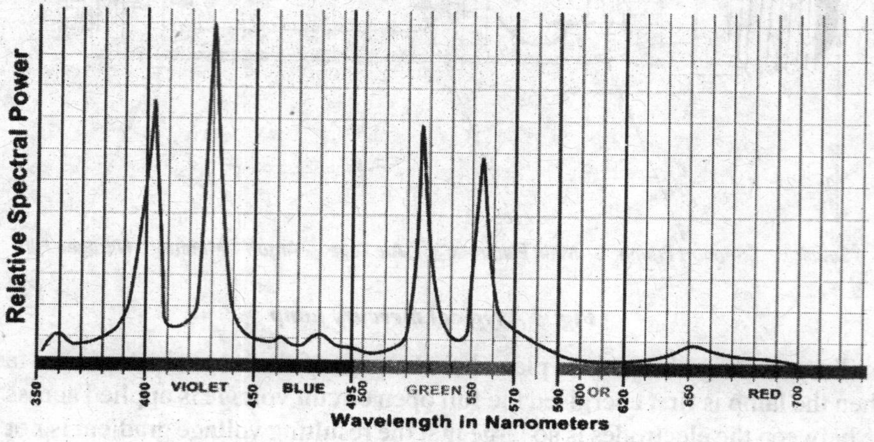

Fig. 4 Mercury vapour lamp spectrum

EXPERIMENT 1

AIM

To determine the wavelength of sodium light by Newton's rings appartatus.

APPARATUS

Monochromatic source of light (sodium lamp), optical arrangements for Newton's rings, spherometer, plano-convex lens of large radius of curvature (~100 cm), travelling microscope, reading lens, glass plate.

THEORY

When a plano-convex lens of large focal length is placed on a plane glass plate with its convex surface in contact with glass plate, a thin film of air is formed between the upper surface of plane glass plate and the lower (convex) surface of lens. When a beam of light from a monochromatic source is made to fall normally on the combination of plano-convex lens and plane glass plate, concentric rings are observed at the of point of contact of the lens and the plate. The fringes are circular because the air film has a circular symmetry. These are known as Newton's rings. These rings are formed due to the interference between the waves reflected from the top and bottom surfaces of the air film. The experimental arrangement is shown in Fig 1.1 and the rings formed (by reflected light) are shown in Fig. 1.2.

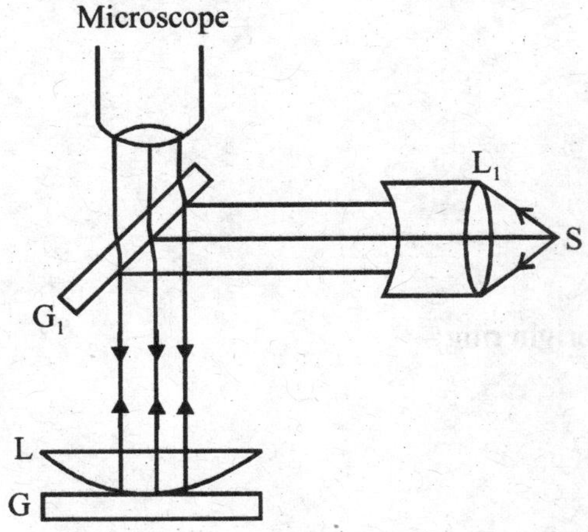

Fig. 1.1 Formation of Newton's Ring

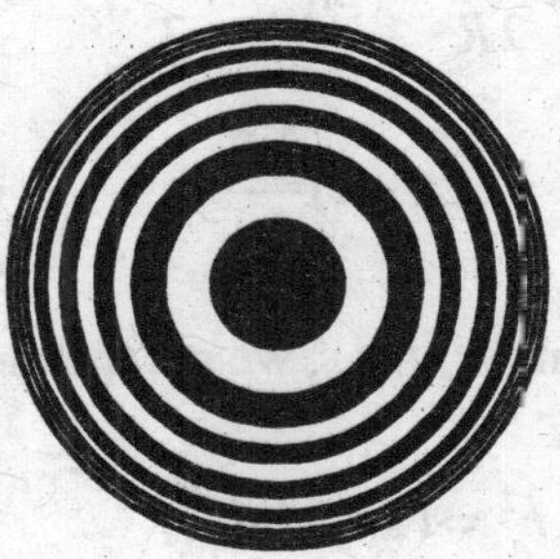

Fig. 1.2 Newton's rings in reflected system

Diameter of Bright and Dark Rings: Consider a plano-convex lens is placed on the glass plate with O is the point of contact, as shown in Fig. 1.3. Let R be the radius of curvature of the lens and t be the thickness of the film at a certain point P. From the property of a circle

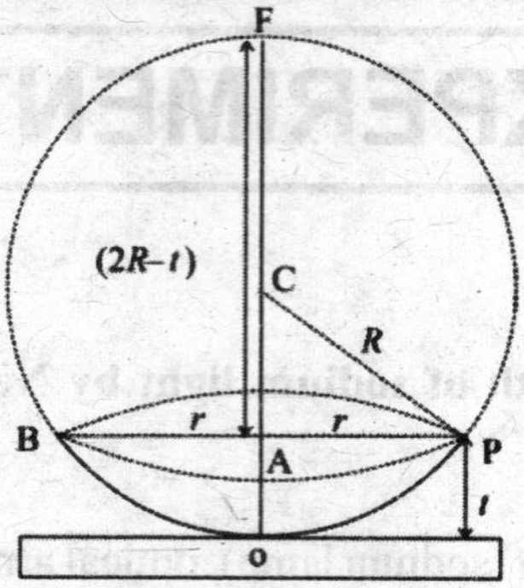

Fig. 1.3

$$AP \times AB = OA \times AF$$

But $AP=AB=r$ (the radius of the ring passing through P), and $OA=PH=t$.

$$\therefore \quad r^2 = t(2R-t) = 2Rt - t^2$$

In actual practice, R>>t. Therefore, t^2 can be neglected in comparison with $2Rt$.

$$\therefore \quad r^2 = 2Rt \text{ or } t = \frac{r^2}{2R}.$$

(i) For maximum intensity or for a bright ring, the condition is, $2\mu t = (2n-1)\frac{\lambda}{2}$

$$\text{or } 2\mu \frac{r^2}{2R} = (2n-1)\frac{\lambda}{2}$$

$$\text{or } r^2 = (2n-1)\frac{\lambda R}{2\mu}.$$

Writing r_n for r, we get the radius of the *n*th bright ring

$$r_n^2 = (2n-1)\frac{\lambda R}{2\mu}.$$

If D_n is the diameter of the nth bright ring, we have

$$\left(\frac{D_n}{2}\right)^2 = (2n-1)\frac{\lambda R}{2\mu}$$

or $D_n^2 = 2(2n-1)\dfrac{\lambda R}{\mu}$.

For air film, $\mu = 1$, therefore $D_n^2 = 2(2n-1)\lambda R$ ...(1.1)

For minimum intensity or for a dark ring, the condition is $2\mu t = n\lambda$

$$\therefore \quad 2\mu\frac{r^2}{2R} = n\lambda \text{ or } r_n^2 = \frac{n\lambda R}{\mu} \text{ or } D_n^2 = \frac{4n\lambda R}{\mu}$$

For air film $\mu = 1$, therefore $D_n^2 = 4n\lambda R$ ...(1.2)

Newton's rings apparatus can be used to determine the wavelength of monochromatic light by measuring the diameter of the dark rings.

If the lens and the glass plate are not quite in contact at the centre of the ring system, as may occur if the surfaces are not clean, the centre may not be dark. To eliminate the error due to this the diameter of any two dark rings nth and (*n*+*m*)th is determined. Thus

$$D_n^2 = 4n\lambda R, \text{ and } D_{n+m}^2 = 4(n+m)\lambda R$$

$$\text{or } \lambda = \frac{D_{n+m}^2 - D_n^2}{4mR} \qquad \text{...(1.3)}$$

This formula involves the difference of the squares of the diameters of two rings and is independent of the thickness of the air film at the so called point of contact.

WORKING FORMULA

The wavelength of monochromatic (sodium) light is given by

$$\lambda = \frac{D_{n+m}^2 - D_n^2}{4mR}$$

where D_n and D_{n+m} are the diameters of nth and (*n*+*m*)th dark rings. *R* is the radius of curvature of plano-convex lens given by

$$R = \frac{l^2}{6h} + \frac{h}{2}$$

where *l* is the mean distance etween the legs of spherometer and *h* is difference of the readings of spherometer on plane glass plate and curved surface of the lens.

PROCEDURE

1. Level the microscope table and set the microscope tube in a vertical position. Find the vernier constant of the horizontal scale.

2. Clean the surface of the plane glass plate P and the plano convex lens L. Place them in position as shown in Fig. 1.1. Place the arrangement in front of a sodium lamp so that the height of the centre of the glass plate G_1 is the same as that of the centre of the sodium lamp. Place the screen in between having a hole of about one inch square in it at the same height. Place the convex lens in between and adjust its position so that a parallel beam of light is made to fall on the glass plate G_1 inclined at an angle of 45°.
3. Adjust the position of microscope so that it lies vertically above the centre of the lens L. Focus the microscope, so that alternate dark and bright rings (as shown in Fig. 1.2) are clearly visible.
4. Adjust the position of the microscope till the point of inter-section of the cross-wire coincides with the centre of the ring system and one of the cross-wires is perpendicular to the horizontal scale.
5. Slide the microscope to the left till the cross-wire lies tangentially at the centre of the 20th dark ring. Note the reading on the vernier scale of the microscope. Slide the microscope backward with the help of the slow motion screw and note the readings when the cross-section wire lies tangentially at the centre of the 16th, 12th, 8th and 4th dark rings respectively.
6. Keep on sliding the microscope to the right and note the reading when the cross wire again lies tangentially at the centre of the 4th, 8th, 12th, 16th and 20th dark rings respectively.
7. After reaching the 20th ring slide the microscope backwards and again note the readings corresponding to the same rings on the right and then to the left of the centre of the ring system.
8. Remove the lens L and find the radius of curvature of the surface of the lens in contact with the glass plate P accurately using a spherometer.

OBSERVATIONS

One division of main scale x = ...cm

No. of division on the vernier scale n=....

Least count of the vernier of the travelling microscope $\frac{x}{n}$ = ...cm

Table 1: Measurements of the diameter of the rings

No. of ring n	*Microscope reading*						Diameter $D = a - b$ (cm)	D^2 (cm^2)	$D^2_{n+m} - D^2_n$ (cm^2)
	Left hand side			*Right hand side*					
	MSR (cm)	*VSR (cm)*	*Total (a) (cm)*	*MSR (cm)*	*VSR (cm)*	*Total (b) (cm)*			
20									
16									
12									
8									
4									

Mean $D^2_{n+m} - D^2_n$ = ... cm².

Measurement of l: Distance between the two legs of the spherometer

$$l_1 = ...cm, l_2 = ...cm, l_3 = ...cm$$

$$l = \frac{l_1 + l_2 + l_3}{3} = ...cm$$

Measurement of h:

Pitch of the screw x = ...cm

No. of divisions on the scale n = ...cm

Least count of the spherometer $\frac{x}{n} = ...cm$

Table 2. Measurements of *h*.

S.No.	*Spherometer reading*						*Difference* $h = a - b$
	Curved surface			*Plane glass plate*			
	MSR (cm)	*CSR (cm)*	*Total(a) (cm)*	*MSR (cm)*	*CSR (cm)*	*Total(b) (cm)*	*(cm)*
1.							
2.							
3.							

Mean h = ... cm.

CALCULATIONS

Radius of curvature of convex surface $R = \frac{l^2}{6h} + \frac{h}{2} = ...$ cm.

Therefore, wavelength $\lambda = \frac{D^2_{n+m} - D^2_n}{4mR} = ...$ cm

RESULT

Mean wavelength of sodium light = ... cm = ... Å

Standard value = 5893Å or 5896 Å

Percentage error =....

PRECAUTIONS AND SOURCES OF ERROR

1. Source of light should be broad extended one.
2. Cross wire of the eye piece must be focussed tangentially on the ring.

3. Plano-convex lens should be of large radius of curvature.
4. The glass plate surface and the lens surface must be cleaned otherwise the rings will not be sharp and bright.

VIVA-VOCE

Q.1 What are Newton's rings?

Ans. Newton rings are alternate bright and dark concentric rings formed in the air film between a plane glass plate and curved surface of plano-convex lens, when illuminated it from the above by a broad extended source of monochromatic light.

Q.2 Why are these rings circular?

Ans. These rings are foci of constant thickness of the air film and these foci being concentric circle hence frings are circular.

Q.3 Why do the rings get closer as the order of the rings increases?

Ans. This is due to the fact that the radii of dark rings are proportional to square root of natural numbers while those of bright rings are proportional to the square root of odd natural numbers and the width of rings decreases as natural number increases.

Q.4 Why is the centre of Newton's rings dark?

Ans. The thickness of air film at the point of contact of glass plate with lens is zero but the interfering waves at the point of contact are opposite in phase, so dark fringe is formed.

Q.5 Sometimes the center is bright. Why?

Ans. This happen when a dust particle comes between the two surfaces at the point of contact.

Q.6 What will happen when the plane glass plate is replaced by plane mirror?

Ans. No fringes will be visible with the plane mirror as the fringes formed by the transmitted light will be superimposed over the fringes formed by the reflected light and uniform illumination will be produced.

Q.7 Can we observe Newton's ring in transmitted light also?

Ans. Yes

Q.8 In transmitted light, is the central spot bright or dark?

Ans. Bright, both patterns (reflected and transmitted) are complementary to each other.

❑❑❑

EXPERIMENT 2

AIM

To determine the dispersive power of material of prism with the help of spectrometer.

APPARATUS

A spectrometer, spirit level, prism, an-eye-piece and mercury lamp.

THEORY

When a ray of white light passes through a prism, it splits into its constituent colours. The phenomenon of splitting of white light into its constituent colours is called dispersion.

The angle through which a ray deviates on passing through a thin prism of small refracting angle A is given by

$$\delta = (\mu - 1) A \qquad \text{....(2.1)}$$

where A is refractive index of material of prism.

This angle of deviation depends upon angle of prism, angle of incidence and material of prism. Variation of angle of deviation δ with angle of incidence i is as shown in fig. 2.1(b)

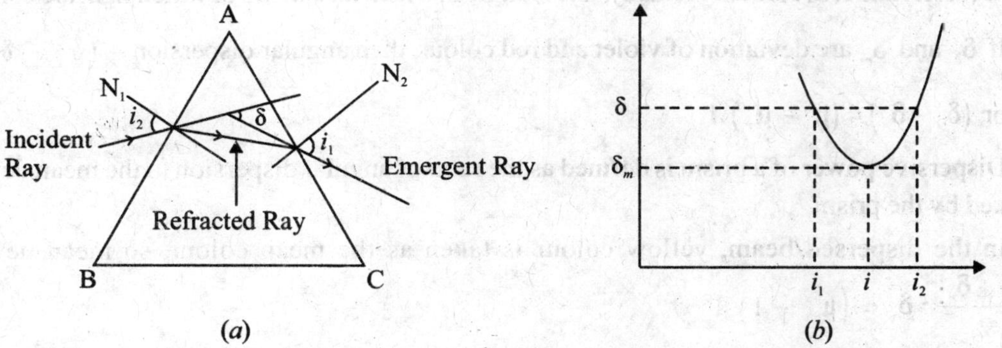

Fig. 2.1(a) Deviation of light ray after passing through prism, (b) Variation of angle of deviation with angle of incidence

When i increase, δ decreases, reaches a minimum and increases again. For one value of δ, there are two angles of incidence i_1 and i_2. However, at minimum deviation $\delta = \delta_m$, $i_1 = i_2$ i.e. the incident ray and the emergent ray are symmetrical w.r.t. the refracting faces. The refracted ray in this case will be parallel to the base.

If μ is the refractive index of the material of the prism,

Then $$\mu = \frac{\sin\left(\frac{A+\delta_m}{2}\right)}{\sin\left(\frac{A}{2}\right)} \quad \text{....(2.2)}$$

This is called prism formula.

Dispersion of Light: Since, each colour has its own characteristic wavelength λ and according to Cauchy's formula, refractive index μ of a material depends on wavelength λ as

$$\mu = A + \frac{B}{\lambda^2} + \frac{C}{\lambda^4} + ... \quad \text{....(2.3)}$$

where *A, B* and *C* are constant

This is μ of a prism is different for different colours and so, from equation (2.1), its is clear that different colours deviate through different angles on passing through the prism. This is the cause of dispersion.

$$\because \quad \lambda_{violet} < \lambda_{red} \Rightarrow \mu_{violet} > \mu_{red} \Rightarrow \delta_{violet} > \delta_{red}$$

i.e. maximum deviation is of violet colour and minimum deviation is of red colour.

The another dispersion produced by a prism is the difference in the angles of deviation of two extreme (violet and red) colours. Actually, this is angle in which all colours of which light are contained.

If δ_v and δ_r are deviation of violet and red colour, then angular dispersion = $(\delta_v - \delta_r)$

or $$(\delta_v - \delta_r) = (\mu_v - \mu_r)A \quad \text{....(2.4)}$$

Dispersive power of a prism is defined as the ratio of angular dispersion to the mean deviation produced by the prism.

In the dispersed beam, yellow colour is taken as the mean colour, so mean deviation $\delta = \frac{\delta_v + \delta_r}{2} = \delta_y = (\mu_y - 1)A$

Thus, dispersive power, $$\omega = \frac{\text{angular dispersion}}{\text{mean deviation}}$$

$$= \frac{(\delta_v - \delta_r)}{\delta_y} = \frac{(\mu_v - \mu_r)A}{(\mu_y - 1)A} = \frac{\mu_v - \mu_r}{(\mu_y - 1)}$$

This is expression for dispersive power of prism. It depends only on nature of material of prism.

WORKING FORMULA

The dispersive power of prism is given by,

$$\omega = \frac{\mu_v - \mu_r}{(\mu_y - 1)}$$

where μ_v and μ_r are the refractive indices for violet and red colours and μ_y is that for the yellow colour, generally taken to be the mean of red and violet colours.

PROCEDURE

To obtain pure spectrum by spectrometer the following adjustments must be made-

1. Adjustment of Collimator :

(i) It consists of a tube mounted horizontally on the arm of spectrometer. The purpose of collimator is to produce a parallel beam of light. The type has a converging achromatic terms at one end. The focal length of lens is equal to the length of collimator tube.

(ii) The vertical slit consists of two sharp edges, which of them one is fixed and other can be moved parallel to it with the help of a screw.

(iii) Finally keep the collimator slit near the window of source.

2. Adjustment of Prism Table :

(i) The prism table has three levelling screws attached to its base. The prism table is made horizontal with the help of spirit level and leveling screws.

(ii) The height of prism table can be adjusted by a clamping screw.

(iii) Now the position of table can be read by verniers moving on the circular scales.

3. Adjustment of Telescope :

(i) The telescope is turned towards an illuminated source of light.

(ii) Now see through the eye piece and then adjust the distance between object and eye piece and get a well defined image of object at the cross wires. The cross wire should be kept horizontal vertical.

(iii) Thus in first arrangement, the telescope is focused for parallel rays while in second, the collimator produces a beam of parallel rays.

4. Measurement of the Angle of Prism

(i) Place the prism on prism table with its refracting edge at the centre and ground face perpendicular to the collimator axis as shown in fig. 2.2

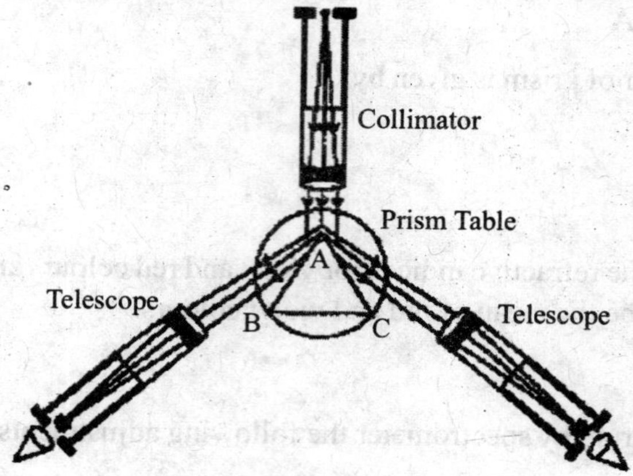

Fig. 2.2 Determination of angle of prism

(ii) The reflected light from each face of prism gives an image of the slit. See the reflected light from face on the right side. Fix the cross wire on this image and note the reading of both verniers.

(iii) Similarly get an image of slit on the left side formed by reflection of light from the order face of the prism and note the reading of both verniers.

(iv) The difference of these two angles will double (i.e. $2A$) of prism angle.

(v) Repeat the process several times and find mean value of A.

5. Measurement of Angle of Minimum Deviation

(i) Place the prism symmetrically at the centre of prism table with it ground face away form collimator.

(ii) Set the telescope at about 45° to axis of collimator. Now rotate prism table towards left or right through a very small angle to make a small angle to normal. Hence on turning the telescope the spectrum will seen.

(iii) With rotating the prism table, spectrum will also rotate. Move the telescope also to keep the spectrum in the field of view. A stage comes when the spectrum just starts returning back. This position is minimum deviation position. At this stage clamp the prism table. In spectrum different colours are in the orders VIBGYOR.

(iv) Now turn the telescope and set its cross wire on red line of spectrum. Now set the cross wire on this line and note the reading of both the verniers. Similarly set the cross wire on different colurs line i.e. yellow, violet respectively and note the readings.

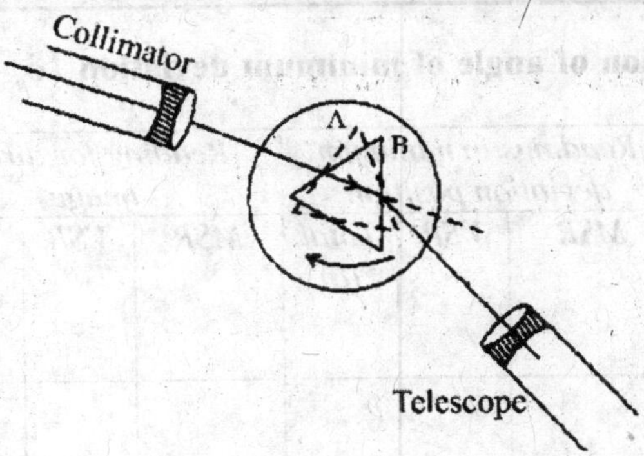

Fig. 2.3 Determination of angle of minimum deviation

(v) Remove the prism from the prism table and turn telescope to obtain direct image. Set the telescope in front of collimator as the cross wire coincide with image of slit. Note the readings of both verniers.

OBSERVATIONS

One division of main scale reading x =.........

No. of division of vernier scale reading n =.........

Least count of vernier scale $\frac{x}{n}$ = ...

Table 1: Determination of angle of prism (A)

S.No.	Vernier	Telescope reading for reflection from face AB			Telescope reading for reflection from face AC			Difference 2A = (a-b)	Mean value 2A
		MSR	VSR	Total (a)	MSR	VSR	Total (b)		
1.	V_1 V_2								
2.	V_1 V_2								

Angle of prism A = ...degree

Table 2: Determination of angle of minimum deviation (δ_m)

S.No.	Colour of spectral line	Scale	Readings in minimum deviation position			Reading for direct image			$\delta_m = a - b$	Mean δ_m
			MSR	VSR	Total (a)	MSR	VSR	Total (b)		
1.	Red	V_1 V_2								
2.	Yellow	V_1 V_2								
3.	Violet	V_1 V_2								

CALCULATIONS

Angle of Prism, A = ...degree

The refractive index for different colours is given by $\mu_v = \dfrac{\sin\left(\dfrac{A+\delta_m}{2}\right)}{\sin\dfrac{A}{2}}$

For violet colour, μ_v = ...

For red colour, μ_r = ...

For yellow colour, μ_y = ...

Dispersive power of prism's material $\omega = \dfrac{\mu_v - \mu_R}{\mu_Y - 1} = \ldots$

Dispersive power of crown glass $\omega_{st} = 0.015$

% error $= \dfrac{\omega_{st} - \omega_{ob}}{\omega_{st}} \times 100\%$

RESULT

The dispersive power of prism's material is......and % error =.......%.

PRECAUTIONS AND SOURCES OF ERROR

1. The telescope should be focused for infinity and the collimator should be adjusted to give a paralleled beam of light.
2. The axis of telescope and collimator, and the plane of prism table should be horizontal.
3. The slit should be as narrow as possible.
4. The telescope should be used on both verniers to note the readings.
5. The circular scale table should be kept fixed during experiment.

VIVA VOCE

Q.1 What do you mean by dispersion?

Ans. When a white light passes through a prism, it is separated into rays of its constituent colours. This phenomenon is known as dispersion.

Q.2 What is angle of deviation?

Ans. The angle between the incident ray and the emergent ray of light is known as the angle of deviation?

Q.3 What is the use of collimator in the spectrometer?

Ans. The collimator makes the light rays coming from the light source parallel to each other.

Q.4 What is the angle of prism?

Ans. The angle between the refracting surfaces of the prism is called angle of prism.

Q.5 Which prism (out of crown and flint glasses) is used for better dispersion?

Ans. Flint glass, because $\omega_f > \omega_c$.

Q.6 What do you mean by angular dispersion?

Ans. Angular dispersion of any two colours (wavelength) is the difference between the deviations of those wavelengths (colours).

Q.7 Can any other device also disperse the light?

Ans. Yes, the diffraction grating also disperse white light.

Q.8 What is the best source of light for determining dispersive power of prism?

Ans. Neon lamp, because it emits the light in all regions of the visible spectrum.

Q.9 How does a ray pass through a prism at minimum deviation?

Ans. Inside the prism the ray passes parallel to the base of the prism.

Q.10 Does the deviation depend on the angle of prism?

Ans. Yes, greater the angle of prism more is the deviation.

Q.11 Does the deviation depends on the colours?

Ans. Yes, the deviation is less for red than for violet light.

Q.12 What is eye-piece?

Ans. Eye-piece is a magnifier designed to give more perfect image obtained by a single lens.

Q.13 Will the angle of minimum deviation change, if the prism is immersed in water.

Ans. Yes, the refractive index of glass in water is less than in air. Hence, the angle of minimum deviation is less.

Q.14 How does refractive index μ vary with wavelength?

Ans. Higher is the wavelength, smaller is the refractive index.

□□□

EXPERMENT 3

AIM

To determine the specific rotation of sugar solution by Bi-quartz or Laurent half shade polarimeter.

APPARATUS

Polarimeter, sodium lamp (for Laurent's half shade polarimeter), table lamp (for biquartz polarimeter), analytical balance, glucose, measuring cylinder, weight box, beaker.

THEORY

Specific Rotation: For a comparison of optical activity, a term specific rotation or specific rotatory power is adopted which is denoted by '*S*'. It is defined differntly for solids, liquids and solutions.

For **solids**; it is defined as:

$$\theta = S \times \ell \qquad ...(3.1)$$

where θ is rotation produced in degrees by ℓ mm length of the solid.

For **liquids**; it is defined as:

$$\theta = S \times \ell \times d \qquad ...(3.2)$$

For **solutions;** for example, sugar dissolved in distilled water, it is defined as:

$$\theta = S \times \ell \times C \qquad ...(3.3)$$

where θ is rotation produced in degrees, ℓ is length of the solution in dm, and C is concentration in gm/cc.

Thus $$S = \frac{\theta}{\ell \times C} = \frac{\text{rotation in degrees}}{\text{length in decimeter} \times \text{concingm/cc}}$$

$$S = \frac{\theta}{\ell \times \left(\frac{m}{v}\right)} = \frac{\theta V}{\ell m} \text{ degree(decimeter)}^{-1} \text{(gm/cc)}^{-1}$$

where *m* is the mass of an optically active substance in gm, '*V*' is the volume of the solution. It is to be pointed out that specific rotation is not a constant, but it varies with the wavelength of light, nature of the active solvent, the concentration of the solution and its temperature.

The product of specific rotation and the molecular weight of an optically active substance is called the molecular rotation. If a plane polarised beam of white light is passed through an optically active solution then light of different wavelengths will have their plane of polarisation rotated by different amount. This phenomenon is called rotatory dispersion.

Polarimeter: It is a device which measures the angle, through which the plane of polarisation of a plane polarised beam is rotated by a given medium. It is also known as saccharimeter when it is used to determine the amount of sugar in a solution.

Construction: The specific rotation of an optically active substance can be calculated by determining the angle of rotation of polarised light.

The polarimeter has three main parts (i) Polariser (ii) a glass tube containing optically active solution or liquid (iii) analyser with circular scale and eye-piece. The arrangement of different parts of the polarimeter is shown in fig. 3.1

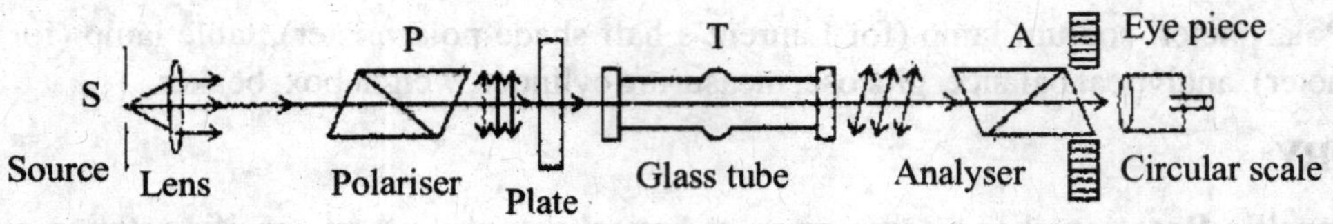

Fig. 3.1 Experimental arrangement

(i) Polariser 'P': It is a Nicol prism or polaroid which is kept stationary. The Nicol prism changes the nincident unpolarised light coming from a source S into plane polarised light. It is arranged in such a way that the plane of vibration of the transmitted light ray is vertical.

(ii) Glass Tube 'T': Optically active solution or liquid whose angle of rotation of the plane polarised light is to be measured is kept in a glass tube. Both ends of the glass tube are covered with two parallel glass plates (cover slips). When plane polarised light passes through this liquid, the vertical plane of vibration is rotated, its position is measured by an analyser. The middle portion of the glass tube has a larger diameter because, if there is any air bubble in the liquid; it will move towards the upper portion of the wider part of the tube and will not come in the way of light.

(iii) Analyser 'A': It is also a Nicol Prism or polaroid which can be rotated about the incident light. For the determination of its angular position, a circular scale with a vernier is attached with the analyser. The transmitted light through the analyser is seen by an eye-piece attached to one end of it.

Working: In order to find the angle of rotation, fill the polarimeter tube with pure water and place the tube in its position inside the polarimeter. Now the analyser is rotated until the intensity of light as seen through the eye-piece becomes zero or the analyzer is in a crossed position and the reading is noted on the circular scale. Now the polarimeter tube is filled with the solution or liquid and placed inside the polarimeter. This optically active liquid or solution rotates the plane of vibration of the polarised light. As a result the intensity of light reappers, when seeing through the eye-piece. Now the analyser is rotated until the intensity of light as seen through the eye-piece becomes zero. The position of analyser is again noted. The difrerence of the two positions of the analyser gives the angle of rotation of the plane of polarisation of the polarised light produced by an optically active solution. This polarimeter is called simple polarimeter. It is less sensitive since at the crossed position of polariser and analyser, even if we rotate the analyser through 4°–5°, the intensity of light is seen almost minimum, hence the angle of rotation cannot be measured accurately. In order to increase the sensitivity of the polarimeter, a particular device is placed between the polariser P and tube T. On the basis of this particular device, the polarimeters are classified into two categories.

There are two main types of polarimeters: (i) Laurent's Half shade polarimeter, (ii) Biquartz polarimeter.

WORKING FORMULA

Sugar solution is dextro-rotatory, i.e. it rotates the plane of polarisation of plane polarised light in clockwise direction. The specific roration $[S]_\lambda^t$ at a given temperature t and for a given wavelength λ is given by

$$[S]_\lambda^t = \frac{\theta}{l \times C}$$

where θ is angle of rotation in degrees, l is length of polarimeter tube in decimeter and C is concentration of solution in gm/cc.

PROCEDURE

1. Weight about 20 gm sugar and dissolve it into 100 c.c. water.
2. Filter the sugar solution with the filter paper if it is not clear.
3. Fill clean polarimeter tube with distilled water such that no air is enclosed in it. If their remains a small air bubble, then the bubble is brought in the bubble trap while placing the tube inside the polarimeter.
4. Place the tube between polariser and the analyser properly.
5. Switch on the sodium lamp (Laurent's half. shade polarimeter) or table lamp (biquartz polarimeter). Look through the analyser and rotate it clockwise till the two halves of the field of view are of the same intensity. This position is such that slight rotation one on half dark and the half bright and slight rotation in the opposite direction will make first half bright and the other half dark as shown in fig. 3.2

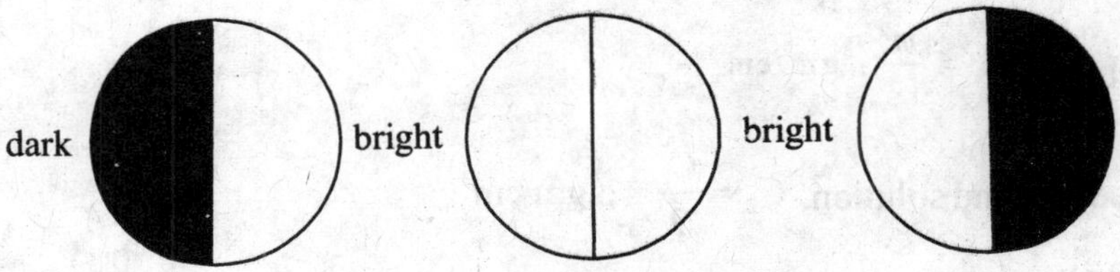

Fig. 3.2 Field of view in Laurent half shade polarimeter

In the polarimeter with biquartz plate, two semicircular parts appear of different colur. The analyser is rotated till first half part appear pink (red) and the second half appears sky (blue) colours shown in fig. 3.3

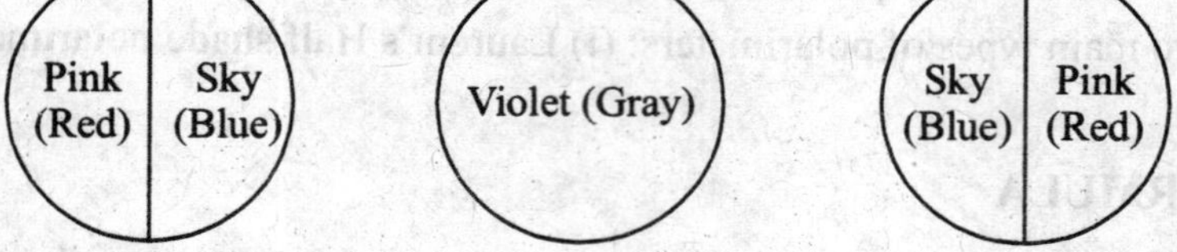

Fig. 3.3 Field of view in Biquartz polarimeter

- Now the analyser is turned gradually with the help of tangential screw till the position of tint of passage appear where yellow height is quenched and sky (blue) and pink (red) colours overlap and both halves of the field of view appear violet (grey). If the analyser is further turned by 1° or 2°, the colours of both halves must again differe but in reverse order.

6. Take the reading of the analyser. Rotate the analyser further in the clockwise direction by about 180° and similar adjustment is again obtained. Note down the reading of the analyser.
7. Now rotate the analyser in the anticlockwise direction and note down the two similar readings for the illumination of the field of view.
8. Remove the water from the polarimeter tube and fill up with prepared solution. Adjust again in the clockiwise and anti clockwise direction and observations are taken as in the case of water.
9. Take 10 cm³ of the above solution in measuring cylinder and add water to make it 20 cm³ solution. The concentration of this second solution will be just half of the previous one. Repeat the observations as described above for this solution.
10. Repeat step 9 again and take observations for the third solution of about 1/4 concentration of the initial one.

OBSERVATIONS

Mass of glucose, $m =$ .... gm.

Initial volume of solution, $V_1 =$.... cm³.

Initial concentration $C_1 = \frac{m}{V_1}$....gm/cm³

Concentration of second solution, $C_2 = \frac{C_1}{2} =$...gm/cm³

Concentration of third solution, $C_3 = \frac{C_1}{4} =$...gm/cm³

Length of polarimeter tube $\ell =$ ....decimeter

one division of main circular scale $x =$ ....degree.

Total no of division in verier scale $n =$ ....

Least count $\frac{x}{n} =$ .... degree.

Table 1: Measurement of angle of rotation

Concentration of the solution (gm/cc)	*First position of the analyzer*			*Position of analyzer after rotating by 180°*			*Mean* $a_1 + b_1)/2$	*Angle of rotation*
	CSR	*VSR*	*Total* (a_1)	*CSR*	*VSR*	*Total* (b_1)		
Pure water							$\theta =$	
C_1=...gm/cc							$\theta_i =$	$\theta_1 = \theta_i - \theta$ = ...
C_2=...gm/cc							$\theta_s =$	$\theta_2 = \theta_s - \theta$ = ...
C_3=...gm/cc							$\theta_t =$	$\theta_3 = \theta_t - \theta$ = ...

CALCULATIONS

1. Concentration of initial/first solution C_1 = ...gm/cm³

   Angle of rotation θ_1 = ...degree

   $$\therefore \text{ specific rotation, } S_1 = \frac{\theta_1}{\ell C_1} = ... \frac{\text{degree} \times \text{cm}^3}{(\text{dm} \times \text{gm})}$$

2. Similarly for second and third solution.

RESULT

The specific rotation of glucose is ...... $\dfrac{\text{degree} \times \text{cm}^3}{(\text{dm} \times \text{gm})}$

Standard value of specific rotation of glucose at 20° C = 52.5 $\dfrac{\text{degree} \times \text{cm}^3}{(\text{dm} \times \text{gm})}$

Percentage error = ...%

PRECAUTIONS AND SOURCES OF ERROR

1. There should be no air bubble in the solution contained in the polarimeter tube.
2. The tube must be rinsed by each solution before it is filled in the tube.
3. Solution must be pure glucose solution in dust free distilled water.

VIVA–VOCE

Q.1 What is polarised light ?

Ans. The light in which the vibrations of electric vector are confined in a definite direction (plane) or directions by any mean, is called polarized light.

Q.2 What is polarization?

Ans. The property of light by virtue of which the plane of vibrations of waves is limits in one particular direction at right angle to the direction of propagation of waves is defined as polarisation.

Q.3 What are different types of polarized light?

Ans. There are three types of polarized light.

These are :

(i) Plane polarized light : the vibrations are along parallel straight lines.

(ii) Circularly polarized light : the vibrations are along a circle.

(iii) Elliptically polarized light : the vibrations ae along an ellipse.

Q.4 Define plane of polarization and plane of vibration?

Ans. The plane containing the direction of vibrations and the direction of propagation is called the plane of vibration, i.e., the plane in which the vibrations take place.

The plane passing through the direction of propagation and containing no vibratons called the plane of polarization.

Q.5 Does the sound wave exhibit polarization?

Ans. Polarization is a property of transverse waves. Sound are longitudinal waves so sound waves do not exhibit polarization.

Q.6 What are ordinary and extraordinary rays?

Ans. When a ray of ordinary light is incident on a calcite crystal, it splits into two refracted ray inside the crystal. Out of the two refracted rays, one obeys the laws of refraction and the other does not. The former is called ordinary. The ordinary ray travels with the same velocity in all direction while the extra ordinary ray travels with different velocity in different directions. The ordinary ray is plane polarized having its plane of vibration perpendicular to the principal section of the crystal i.e. having its plane of polarization in principal section. Whereas, the extra-ordinary ray is plane polarized having its vibrations in principal section i.e. having its plane of polarization perpendicular to the principal section.

Q.7 What is phenomenon of double refraction?

Ans. When ordinary light is incident on a calcite or quartz crystal, its splits in two refracted rays (E-ray & O-ray) and this phenomenon is known as double refraction.

Q.8 Define optic axis and principal section?

Ans. A line passing through any one of the blunt corners and making equal angles with three faces which meet there, is the direction of optic axis. It is the direction along which the two refracted rays (O-ray & E-ray) trave with the same velocity. A plane containing the optic axis and perpendicular to two opposite faces is called the principal section.

Q.9 What is Nicol Prism?

Ans. A device made out of the calcite crystal, with the help of which plane polarised light can be produced and analysed is known a Nicol prism.

Q.10 What is meant by "optically active" substance ?

Ans. A substance which can rotate the plane of polarization of polarised light.

Q.11 Name some of the optically active substances.

Ans. (i) Dextro–rotatory substances are cane–sugar, tartaric acid, camphor, d-glucose and d-quartz.

(ii) Laevo–rotatory substances are fructose, turpentine and ℓ–quartz.

Q.12 Define specific rotation?

Ans. The specific rotation of a substance at a particular temperature and for a given wavelength of light is defined as the rotation produced by one decimeter length of substance of unit concentration. (1m/c.c.); i.e.,

$$\text{Specific Rotation} = S = \frac{\theta}{\ell \times C}$$

where θ is the angle of rotation in degrees, ℓ is the length of substance (or solution) in decimeter and C is the concentration (or density) in gm/cc.

Q. 13 On what factors does specific rotation depend?

Ans. The specific rotation depends upon (i) the wavelength of light, (ii) temperature, (iii) the nature of the inactive solvent, and (iv) the concentration of the solution.

Q. 14 What is polarimeter ?

Ans. Polarimeter is an instrument for measuring the angle of rotation of the plane of vibration of light polarised by an optically active substance.

Q. 15 How does the optical activity depend on the wavelength of the light employed ?

Ans. The amount of rotation is approximately inversely proportional to the square of the wavelength.

Q. 16 What do you mean by the term 'rotatory dispersion'?

Ans. The phenomenon of variation of rotation of plane of polarization with wavelength is known as rotatory dipersion.

❑❑❑

EXPERIMENT 4

AIM

To determine the speed of ultrasonic waves in a liquid by diffraction method.

APPARATUS

A radio frequency oscillator fitted with a frequency meter, a quartz crystal slab fitted with two leads, ultrasonic spectrometer, a glass cell with experimental liquid, a sodium lamp, a convex lens, a spirit level etc.

THEORY

Ultrasonic waves are longitudinal mechanical waves of frequency beyond the highest audible frequency (i.e. 20,000 Hz). One of the important methods of producing ultrasonic waves is piezoelectric oscillator. It makes use of piezoelectric effect exhibited by crystals of quartz, zinc blende, Rochelle salt etc.

When a slab of quartz is subjected to a mechanical pressure on one pair of opposite faces, electric charges are developed on the other pair of parallel faces perpendicular to the first pair. The quantity of charge developed is proportional to the applied pressure. The sign of the charge changes when the pressure is changed into tension. This phenomenon is known as piezoelectric effect. The converse is also true, i.e. when an electric potential difference is applied across the faces of a crystal, the crystal undergoes a strain. If the direction of applied potential difference is reversed the direction of strain is also reversed i.e., if in the first case it is a compression strain now it will be an extension strain and vice versa. Hence if an alternating voltage is applied to the crystal slab along its thickness there are alternating changes in its length and thickness i.e. when the length increases, the thickness increases and vice versa with the same frequency as that of the applied a.c. voltage. This phenomenon is known as inverse piezoelectric effect. When the frequency of the applied a.c. voltage becomes equal to the natural frequency of the slab, resonant vibrations take place in the slab. The natural frequency of vibration of the slab is given by

$$n = \frac{1}{2d}\sqrt{\frac{E}{\rho}}$$

where d is the distance between the opposite faces of the crystal slab, E is the bulk modulus of quartz and ρ is the density of quartz.

The velocity of ultrasonic waves set up in a liquid can be determined with the help of an ultrasonic spectrometer, which is almost similar to an optical spectrometer. The experimental arrangement is shown in Fig. 4.1.

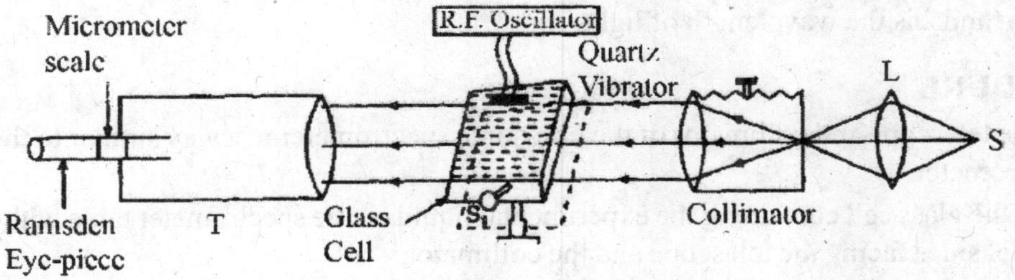

Fig. 4.1 : Experimental arrangement

The ultrasonic waves set up in a liquid form an acoustic grating. When plane ultrasonic waves are produced in a liquid the pressure varies periodically with the distance from the ultrasonic source being higher at a compression and lower at a rarefaction. The density of the medium and the refractive index also show a periodic variation with distance from the source along the direction of propagation of the wave. Under such a condition, if light from a slit is passed through the liquid in a direction at right angles to the wave propagation the liquid behaves as a diffraction grating with grating element equal to the wavelength of ultrasonic wave λ_u. Such a grating is known as acoustic grating. The light which suffers diffraction at this grating shows a number of diffraction images of the slit when seen through a telescope formed at the position of the cross-wire of the telescope eyepiece.

If θ is the angle of diffraction for n^{th} order maxima, then

$$\lambda_u \sin\theta = 2n\lambda \quad \text{...(4.1)}$$

where λ is the wavelength of light used. The factor of 2 arises because the wave contains two compressions and two rarefactions.

Therefore, wavelength of ultrasonic waves, $\lambda_u = \dfrac{2n\lambda}{\sin\theta}$. ...(4.2)

If v is the frequency of ultrasonic waves, then velocity of ultrasonic wave is given by

$$V = \frac{2vn\lambda}{\sin\theta} \quad \text{...(4.3)}$$

For small values of θ, we have $\sin\theta \sim \theta$.

Therefore, $V = \dfrac{2vn\lambda}{\theta}$ ...(4.4)

WORKING FORMULA

The velocity of ultrasonic waves in the liquid is given by

$$V = \frac{2vn\lambda}{\theta}$$

where v is the frequency of ultrasonic waves, θ is the angle of diffraction, n is the order of diffraction and λ is the wavelength of light.

PROCEDURE

1. Set the telescope and collimator of the ultrasonic spectrometer in a way similar to that of optical spectrometer.
2. Place the glass cell containing the experimental liquid on the spectrometer table with its opposite parallel sides facing the telescope and the collimator.
3. Mount the quartz crystal slab in its holder and dip it in the liquid near a wall of the glass cell so that the ultrasonic waves produced by the crystal travel in the liquid in a direction perpendicular to that of the incident light. Connect the leads of the crystal slab with the output terminals of the R.F. oscillator.
4. Switch on the sodium lamp and focus its light on the slit of the collimator. See through the telescope eyepiece so that a sharp well defined image of the slit is seen in the field of view in the centre of the micrometer scale fitted in the eyepiece.
5. Now switch on the R.F. oscillator. Ultrasonic waves are setup in the liquid. Adjust the frequency of the oscillator so that it becomes equal to the natural frequency of the crystal slab. At this range resonance takes place and diffraction images of the slit will be seen in the telescope. Note the frequency of the R.F. oscillator. Maintain it constant at this value throughout the experiment.
6. If the diffraction images are not seen by adjusting the frequency of the oscillator, then readjust the position and orientation of the crystal in the liquid and the position and level of the glass cell.
7. Measure the angle of diffraction of various order diffraction images on both sides from the central zero order image.

OBSERVATIONS

Wavelength of sodium light, $\lambda = 5893 \times 10^{-8}$ cm

Room temperature = ... °C

Frequency of the oscillator used, ν = ... Hz.

Least count of the spectrometer = ... min.

Table 1: Determination of velocity of ultrasonic waves

Sr. No	*Order of diffraction maximum*	*Vernier*	*Position of diffracted image*						*θ = (a – b)/2*
			Left of central image			*Right of central image*			
			Main scale	*Vernier scale*	*Total reading (a)*	*Main scale*	*Vernier scale*	*Total reading (b)*	
1	1	V_1							
		V_2							
2	2	V_1							
		V_2							

CALCULATIONS

First set: For $n = 1$, $V = \frac{2\nu\lambda}{\theta}$ = ...cm/s.

Second set: $n = 2$, $V = \frac{4\nu\lambda}{\theta}$ = ...cm/s.

Mean velocity of ultrasonic waves, V = ... cm/s.

Result: Velocity of ultrasonic waves in the given liquid = ... cm/s.

PRECAUTIONS AND SOURCES OF ERROR

1. The glass cell should be thoroughly cleaned and filled with the liquid filtered a number of times.
2. The crystal slab should be immersed completely in the liquid and should touch neither the bottom nor the side walls.
3. The crystal slab should be set in such a way that the ultrasonic waves produced by it travel at right angles to the incident light.
4. The diffraction pattern should be sharp and narrow.
5. The frequency of the R.F. oscillator should be properly adjusted for resonance and should not be disturbed during the experiment.

VIVA-VOCE

Q. 1. What are ultrasonic?

Ans. Sounds of frequencies beyond 20 kHz are called ultrasonics and those less than 20 Hz are called infrasonics.

Q. 2. What is the audible frequency range of human hair?

Ans. Human ear can hear sound of frequencies between 20 Hz and 20,000 Hz (20 kHz).

Q. 3. What name is given to frequencies below the audible range?

Ans. Infrasonics

Q. 4. Are ultrasonic waves longitudinal or transverse?

Ans. Ultrasonic waves are longitudinal in nature.

Q. 5. Do ultrasonic waves travel faster than sound waves?

Ans. No, sound waves and ultrasonic waves travel with the same speed. However, an object moving with a speed more than that of sound is called a supersonic.

Q. 6. Give some methods of producing ultrasonics.

Ans. Ultrasonics can be produced by magnetostriction effect, Galton's whistle, piezoelectric effect etc.

Q. 7. Give some methods for detection of ultrasonics.

Ans. Ultrasonics can be detected by thermal detectors, Kundt's tube, and piezoelectric materials.

Q. 8. Give the units of measurement of loudness of sound?

Ans. Loudness of sound is measured in decibels (dB).

Q. 9. How decibel differs from Phon?

Ans. Loudness of sound measured by taking some standard frequency (1000 Hz) as unit measures the loudness as Phon. So decibel and Phon scales match the loudness at 1000 Hz and differ from other frequencies.

Q. 10. Why ultrasound scanning is preferred over X-rays for imaging of body parts?

Ans. X-erays may be stopped at some places in body and so will have harmful effects due to radiation phenomenon while ultrasound have no harmful effects on any part of the body.

Q. 11. What is threshold of hearing and what is the maximum limit of hearing?

Ans. Threshold of hearing on decibel (dB) scale is taken as dB while sound rounds beyond 120 dB produce painful effects.

Q. 12. What is piezoelectric effect?

Ans. The phenomenon of development of equal and opposite electric charges (potential difference) on the opposite faces of certain crystal slices cut suitably when they are subjected too mechanical stress is known as piezoelectric effect.

Q. 13. What is inverse piezoelectric effect?

Ans. The phenomenon of change in dimensions of a crystal when a potential difference is applied to its opposite faces is known as inverse piezoelectric effect.

Q. 14. State the formula for frequency of a quartz crystal.

Ans. The frequency of a quartz crystal is given by $V = \frac{2vn\lambda}{\theta}$ where í is the frequency of ultrasonic waves, θ is the angle of diffraction, n is the order of diffraction and λ is the wavelength of light.

Q. 15. What do you understand by acoustic grating?

Ans. When stationary waves are set in the liquid, the density of liquid is maximum at nodes and minimum at antinodes. The arrangement is similar to just to diffraction grating and so is called acoustic grating.

Q. 16. What is the grating element of such a grating?

Ans. The grating element in such a grating is equal to distance between two nodes or antinodes.

❑❑❑

EXPERIMENT 5

AIM

To determine the width of a narrow slit using diode laser by diffraction phenomena.

APPARATUS

Variable single slit, optical bench with uprights, diode laser, two lenses, graph paper, pen etc.

THEORY

When a beam of light passes through a narrow slit, it spreads into the region of the geometrical shadow. This phenomenon of light is known as diffraction and it can be explained only by assuming wave nature of light. The diffraction effects in light are generally classified into two main categories known as Fresnel's diffraction and Fraunhoffer's diffraction. In the Fresnel's class of diffraction either the light source or the screen or both of them are at finite distances from the obstacle or the aperture causing diffraction. In the Fraunhoffer's class of diffraction the light source and screen are effectively at infinite distance from the diffracting aperture or obstacle. In practice, it is achieved by rendering the incoming light into a parallel beam by the use of a collimating lens and focusing the diffracted parallel light beam on the screen by a convergent lens placed on the other side of obstacle or aperture.

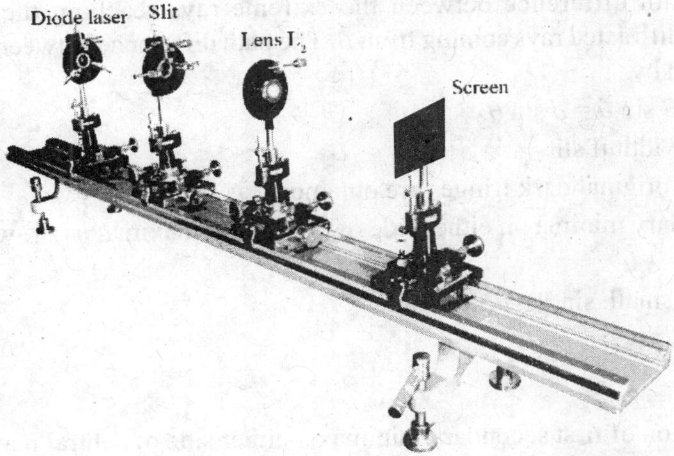

Fig. 5.1 Experimental arrangement

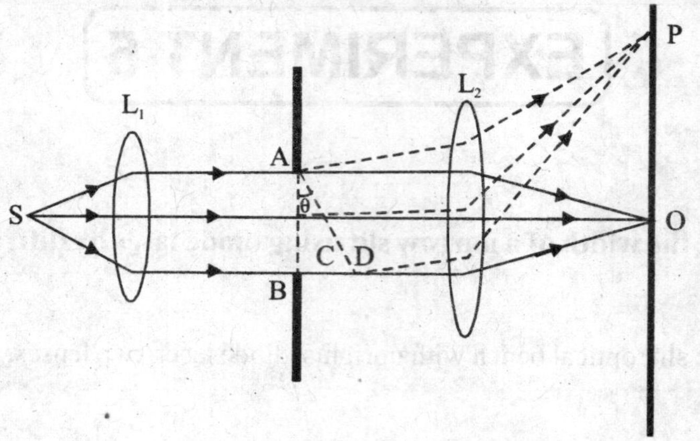

Fig. 5.2 : Ray diagram

An experimental arrangement to determine the width of narrow slit by Fraunhoffer's diffraction pattern is shown in Fig. 5.1. The ray diagram is shown in Fig. 5.2. S is the monochromatic source of light (in this case diode laser) of wavelength λ; L_1 is the collimating lens which effectively places the source at infinite distance. The diffraction pattern due to the single slit is formed at infinity, which is brought into focus by the lens L_2 at the plane of the screen. The waves reaching point O, just opposite the middle of the slit form a bright central image because the secondary waves from points equidistant from C and situated in the upper and lower halves of the wavefront travel the same distances in reaching O and hence the path difference is zero. Let us now find the resultant intensity at any point P above O produced by the rays diffracted at an angle θ. The secondary waves coming from all the points from the slit travel different distances in reaching the point P in different phases. To determine the path difference between the extreme rays reaching the point P, draw AD perpendicular to the diffracted rays coming from B. The path difference between the rays originating from A and B is given by

$$BD = AB \sin\theta = d \sin\theta. \quad ...(5.1)$$

where d is the width if slit.

If $d \sin\theta = n\lambda$, original dark fringes are obtained.

For first secondary minima on either side of the central maxima, $n = 1$, we obtain

$$d \sin\theta = \lambda \quad ...(5.2)$$

When θ is very small, $\sin\theta \sim \theta$, we obtain

$$d = \frac{\lambda}{\theta} \quad ...(5.3)$$

If P is the position of first secondary minima on either side of central maxima, then width of central maxima is given by

$$b = D.2\theta$$

or $\quad \theta = b/D \quad ...(5.4)$

where D is the distance from the plane of the slit to the plane of the screen. Hence

Therefore, measuring the values of D and b from the experimental setup and knowing the value of λ, the width of the slit d can be estimated.

WORKING FORMULA

The width of slit is given by

$$d = \frac{2\lambda D}{b}$$

where D is the distance from the plane of the slit, b is the width of central maxima, and λ is the wavelength of light.

PROCEDURE

1. Take an optical bench with five uprights and level it with the help of a spirit level by adjusting the screws provided at its four corners.
2. Mount the diode laser, lens L_1, slit, lens L_2, and screen on the uprights at same height as shown in Fig. 5.1. Adjust the lens L_1 on one side and L_2 on other side of the slit. If L_2 is very close to the slit, the distance between the slit and screen, D can be taken equal to the focal length of the lens. Adjust the screen at the focal point of lens L_2 so as to observe the diffraction pattern. Paste a graph paper on the screen.
3. Switch on the power supply.
4. Mark the edges of the first minima on either side of the principal maxima on a graph placed on the screen and measure the width of central maxima. To minimize the error, the measurement should be taken at least three times.
5. Take three sets of readings using three different focal lengths for L_2.

OBSERVATIONS

Table 1: Measurement of width of slit

Sr. No.	*Distance between L_2 and screen D (cm)*	*Width of central maxima b (cm)*	*Mean width b (cm)*	*Width of slit $d = 2D\lambda/b$ (cm)*	*Mean d (cm)*
1					
2					
3					

CALCULATIONS

The wavelength of light used, $\lambda = 670 \times 10^{-7}$ cm
Width of slit, $d = 2D\lambda/b = \ldots$ cm = ... mm

RESULT

The width of slit = ... mm

PRECAUTIONS AND SOURCES OF ERROR

1. Slit should be vertical and straight.
2. The laser beam should be collimated properly.
3. Distance between the slit and second lens L_2 should be as small as possible.
4. Readings should be taken repeatedly to minimize measurement error.

VIVA-VOCE

Q. 1. On which phenomenon of light, this experiment is based?
Ans. Diffraction of light
Q. 2. What is diffraction of light?
Ans. When light is made to fall on an obstacle or an aperture having size comparable to the wavelength of light then the light is found to bend round the corners of obstacle or aperture. This bending of light around corners is known as diffraction.
Q. 3. What is the essential difference between interference and diffraction?
Ans. In interference the resultant intensity at a point is obtained due to superposition of wave fronts coming from two coherent sources but in diffraction the resultant intensity at a point is obtained due to the superposition of secondary wavelets of single wave front.
Q. 4. Why laser is used in this experiment. Is it possible to perform the same experiment with white light source?
Ans. In interference and diffraction experiments highly coherent sources are required. Since a laser light is highly coherent and therefore it used to produce diffraction pattern due to a single slit. With white light source, it is not possible to produce this experiment.
Q. 5. How does laser light differ from ordinary light?
Ans. The laser light differs from ordinary light in the following respects: high directionality, highly monochromatic, highly intense, and highly coherent.
Q. 6. What do you mean by the term coherence? What are its types?
Ans. The coherence is a measure of the degree of phase correlation that exists in the radiation field of a light source at different locations and different times. The coherence is of two types: temporal coherence and spatial coherence.
Q. 7. What is an active medium as used in lasers?
Ans. A medium in which light gets amplified is called an active medium, and it may be a gas, a liquid or a solid.

Q. 8. What are various types of lasers in common use?

Ans. Lasers can be classified on the basis of active medium. Ruby laser, Nd:YAG laser, Nd:glass lasers, Ti:sapphire laser etc. are solid state lasers. He-Ne laser, Argon ion laser, CO_2 laser are gas lasers. Diode lasers are semiconductor lasers.

Q. 9. What is population inversion?

Ans. The process by which the population of higher state is appreciably increases as compared to that in the ground state is called population inversion.

Q. 10. What are the main components of a laser?

Ans. The main components of a laser are: an active medium, resonant cavity, and pumping system.

Q. 11. What is the wavelength of diode laser used in this experiment?

Ans. The wavelength of light used in this experiment is 6700 Å.

Q. 12. How the pattern on screen changes with the change in slit width?

Ans. The width of central maxima decreases with increasing slit width.

Q. 13. Why the intensity on the screen decreases as we move away from the central maxima?

Ans. This is due to absorption of light in the air medium.

❑❑❑

EXPERIMENT 6

AIM

To determine the temperature coefficient of resistance for Platinum using a Platinum resistance thermometer and a Callender and Griffith's bridge.

APPARATUS

Callender and Griffith's bridge, Platinum resistance thermometer, galvanometer, hot water bath, cell, plug key, rheostat connecting wires, and mercury thernometer.

THEORY

Platinum Resistance Thermometer: The resistance of an electric conductor is a function of temperature and forms the basis of resistance thermometry. Many of conductors do not offer always the same resistance at a given temperature but the resistance of platinum wire free from impurities is found to be a unique function of temperature. The platinum resistance thermometer is shown in Fig 6.1. Pure platinum wire free from impurities (carbon, silicon, tin and others) double on itself to avoid induction effect, is wound on a thin plate of mica. The ends of the platinum wire are soldered to two thick leads of copper or platinum whose other ends are connected to two terminals *PP* on the top of porcelain tube. Parallel to the thick leads, there are two terminals *CC*. This extra pair of leads is called compensating leads. The function of compensating leads is to eliminate the resistance of the connecting leads to the platinum wire at all temperatures. A number of mica discs are placed in the tube to insulate the leads from each other. This also prevents convection current in the air of the tube.

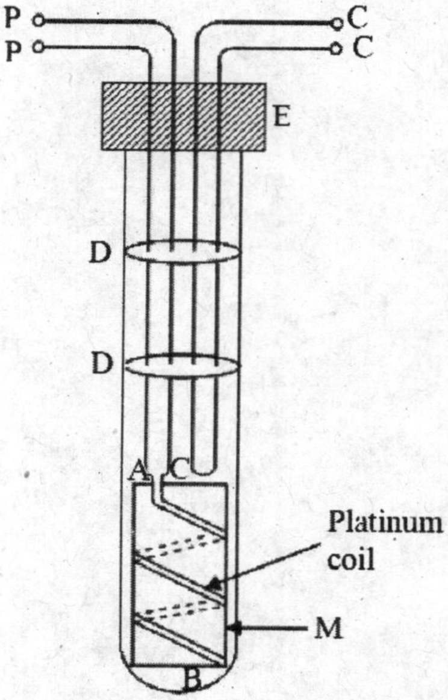

Fig. 6.1 Platinum resistance thermometer

Callender and Griffith's Bridge: For the measurement of the resistance of platinum wire at different temperatures, Callender and Griffith devised a modified form of Wheatstone bridge known as Callender and Griffith's bridge. This is shown in Fig. 6.2.

In the circuit, the ratio arms *P* and *Q* are made equal. The platinum leads are connected in the third arm *S*, while the fourth arm *R* contains coils of different known resistances (marked) 1, 2, ...10 unit etc. (each unit is equivalent to the stretched wire) along with the compensating leads of the thermometer. Between the arms *R* and *S* a uniform resistance wire *MN* of resistance ρ ohm per cm. is connected. A sliding contact *D* moves on the wire *MN*. The battery *B* and galvanometer *G* are also connected.

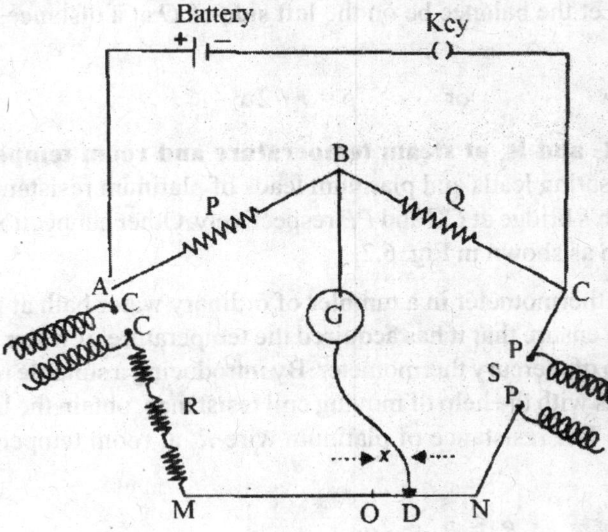

Fig. 6.2. Callender and Griffith's bridge

WORKING FORMULA

Temperature coefficient of resistance, α is given by

$$\alpha = \frac{R_2 - R_1}{R_1 T_2 - R_2 T_1} \text{ per °C}$$

where R_1 and R_2 be the resistances of platinum wire at temperatures T_1 and T_2 respectively. Using a Callender and Griffith's bridge, the resistance, R is given by

$$R = r + 2\rho x$$

where ρ is the resistance per unit length of the potentiometer wire, r is the resistance introduced in resistance box, and x is the distance of null point from middle point (electrical zero). The proper sign is used according as the balance point lies to the right or left of the electrical zero.

PROCEDURE

1. **Determination of Electrical Zero:** Complete the connections as shown in Fig. 5.2. Short circuit the gaps *PP* and *CC*, i.e., connect the terminals by a thick copper wire. Make the resistance *R* zero by moving the key of variable resistance. Now make the cell circuit on by inserting the plug key. Determine the position of null point by moving the jockey on the bridge wire. The null point gives the position of electrical zero. This should be noted down.

2. **Determination of resistance per unit length ñ of the bridge wire:** To determine the value of ρ, the gaps (*PP* and *CC*) are short circuited. The value from *R* is adjusted to a small value *r* to

obtain the balance. Let the balance be on the left side of O at a distance x from the position of electrical zero.

$$0 = r - 2\rho x \qquad \text{or} \qquad \rho = r/2x$$

3. **Determination of R_1 and R_2 at steam temperature and room temperature respectively:** Connect the compensating leads and platinum leads of platinum resistance thermometer to the Callender and Griffith's bridge at *CC* and *PP* respectively. Other connections are made according to the circuit diagram as shown in Fig. 6.2.

   Place the bulb of the thermometer in a tumbler of ordinary water bath at room temperature and wait for some time to ensure that it has acquired the temperature of water. Note the temperature of water with the help of mercury thermometer. By introducing a suitable resistance in the circuit of compensating leads with the help of moving coil resistance, obtain the balance. This length of bridge wire is noted. The resistance of platinum wire R_1 at room temperature is calculated by using the relation:

$$R_1 = R \pm 2\rho x$$

   where R is the resistance introduced in the variable resistance R and x is the length on bridge wire from electrical zero to get the null point.

   Note the platinum resistance thermometer is placed in a hypsometer or in a hot water bath and wait for such time that it acquires the constant temperature of bath. Note this temperature also and determine again the resistance of the platinum wire as described above in the step 2. Let the resistance at this temperature be denoted by R_2.

$$\alpha = \frac{R_2 - R_1}{R_1 T_2 - R_2 T_1}$$

   Calculate the value of α using the relation:

OBSERVATIONS

Table 1: Determination of electrical zero

Sr. No.	*Position of balance point when both PP and CC are shorted (cm)*	*Electrical zero (cm)*	*Mean electrical zero (cm)*
1			
2			
3			
4			

Table 2: Determination of ρ

Sr. No.	Resistance introduced in the moving coil resistance r (ohm)	Distance of null point on bridge wire (cm)	Distance between electrical zero and null point (cm)	$\rho = r/2x$ (ohm/cm)	Mean ρ (ohm/cm)
1					
2					
3					
4					

Table 3: Determination of R_1 and R_2

Sr. No.	Temperature of bath	Reading	Resistance used in coil r (ohm)	Shift of balance from electrical zero x (cm)	Resistance of platinum wire in the thermometer $R = r \pm 2\rho x$ (ohm)	Mean (ohm)
1	Room temperature = ... °C.	2.0			$R_1 =$	$R_1 =$
2		3.0			$R_1 =$	
3						
4						
1	Temperature of boiling water = ...°C.	2.0			$R_2 =$	$R_2 =$
2		3.0			$R_2 =$	
3						
4						

CALCULATIONS

Temperature coefficient of resistance, $\alpha = \dfrac{R_2 - R_1}{R_1T_2 - R_2T_1}$ = ... per °C.

RESULT

The temperature coefficient of resistance for platinum = ... per °C.
The standard value of temperature coefficient of resistance for platinum = 37×10^{-4} per °C.
Percentage error = ... %

PRECAUTIONS AND SOURCES OF ERROR

1. The end of the connection wires as well as surfaces of copper strips should be well cleaned; moreover connections should be made tight.
2. The balance point for the measurement of R_1 and R_2 should be determined only when the temperature acquired by the platinum resistance thermometer are steady.
3. Jockey should be pressed on the bridge wire so as to make proper contact.
4. The jockey should never be kept pressed while it is being moved on the wire.

VIVA-VOCE

Q. 1. Distinguish between temperature and heat.

Ans. The degree of hotness of a body is called temperature. All bodies in thermal contact with each other ultimately attain the same temperature. The flow of energy from one body to another due to a temperature difference between the two is called heat. Two bodies in thermal equilibrium with each other may not have the same amount of heat but they must have the same temperature.

Q. 2. What do you understand by the term thermometer?

Ans. Thermometers are the devices used to measure the temperature of a body with scientific precision.

Q. 3. What is the basic principle of resistance thermometers?

Ans. These are based on the principle of change of electrical resistance with temperature.

Q. 4. Explain the construction and working of platinum resistance thermometer.

Ans. See theory section.

Q.5. What is the function of compensating leads (CC) in the PRT?

Ans. The function of compensating leads is to eliminate the resistance of the connecting leads to the platinum wire at all temperatures.

Q. 6. Define temperature coefficient of resistance.

Ans. The temperature coefficient of resistance may be defined as increase in resistance per unit resistance at 0°C for 1°C rise of temperature.

Q. 7. Is value of temperature coefficient always positive?

Ans. The temperature coefficient has a positive value for metals and alloy. For semiconductors and insulators, its value is negative.

Q. 8. What is the basic principle of Callender and Griffith's bridge?

Ans. It is based on the principle of Wheatstone bridge.

Q. 9. How you will obtain null point in Callender and Griffith's bridge?

Ans. See the procedure of experiment.

Q. 10. How electrical resistance depends upon temperature?

Ans. The electrical resistance of all metals increases with increase of temperature. In case of semiconductors, the resistance decreases with increase of temperature.

Q. 11. For the measurement of temperature coefficient how this apparatus is calibrated?

Ans. See the theory section.

Q. 12. What are the advantages of this experiment?

Ans. It has a wide range from – 200°C to 1200°C. It has good accuracy i.e., it can read accurately up to 0.01°C. At lower temperatures, it is as accurate as a gas thermometer beyond 1000°C on account of the impurity as may come due to combination of insulating materials.

Q. 13. What are the disadvantages of this experiment?

Ans. The container tube has large thermal capacity and low thermal conductivity and so it cannot respond to quick changes of temperatures. Moreover it takes quite some time to get a balance point on the bridge.

❑❑❑

EXPERIMENT 7

AIM

To determine the value of specific charge (*e/m*) of an electron by Thomson's method.

APPARATUS

A cathode ray tube fitted on a wooden stand provided with two arms perpendicular to the axis of the tube and having scales with zero at the point where the central line of the arms cuts the axis of the tube, a power supply unit capable of giving the accelerating d.c. voltage for the cathode ray tube and the deflecting d.c. voltage for the electric field through a reversing key with suitable voltmeters, two bar magnets, a compass box, a compass needle, etc.

THEORY

e/m of an electron: *e/m* of an electron is the ratio of the charge on an electron to its rest mass. It is also known as specific charge and its value is given by

$$e/m = 1.76\times 10^{11} \text{ coulomb/kg} = 1.76\times 10^{7} \text{ e.m.u./gm} = 5.28\times 10^{17} \text{ e.s.u./gm.}$$

The value of *e/m* can be determined by the method originally used by Prof. J.J. Thomson.

The apparatus consists of cathode ray tube (Fig.7.1) which has three essential parts:

(i) **The electron gun:** This part consists of the cathode *K* and anode *A*. It produces, accelerates and focuses the electrons into a fine beam so as to produce a small bright spot on the fluorescent screen *S*.

(ii) **The screen:** The screen *S* is located with some fluorescent material like zinc sulphide etc. so that a greenish blue spot of light is observed where the electron beam impinges upon the screen. A transparent mm graph is attached to the screen to note the exact position of the fluorescent spot.

(iii) **The electric and magnetic deflecting system:** Two plates *P* and *Q* are fitted in the tube symmetrically on either side of the electron beam so that an electric field perpendicular to the plane of the paper can be applied between them.

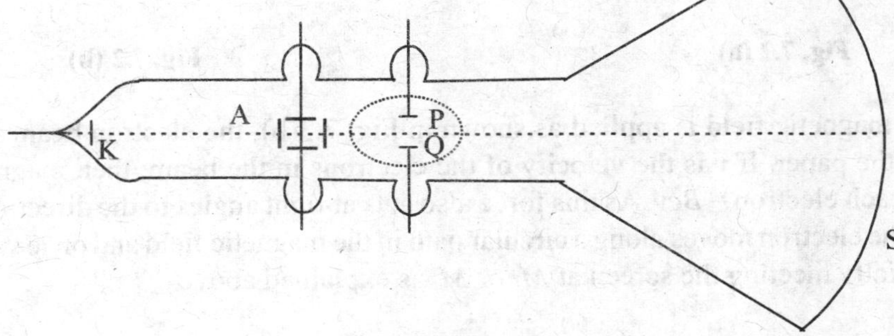

Fig. 7.1 Cathode ray tube

A magnetic field can also be applied at the same place in a direction perpendicular to the direction of the electric field i.e., in the plane of the paper. Thus the deflection of the cathode rays due to the electric as well as the magnetic field takes place in a direction perpendicular to the plane of the paper.

To apply the magnetic field the cathode ray tube is fitted on a wooden stand provided with two arms, one on either side perpendicular to the direction of the electron beam. A scale is marked on each arm which gives the distance from the axis of the cathode ray tube. When two bar magnets are placed with their lengths parallel to the arms with their opposite poles towards the cathode ray tube, these produce a uniform magnetic field exactly at the same place where an electric field is produced when a potential difference is applied between the plates P and Q.

Let E be the intensity of the electric field applied between the plates P and Q in a direction perpendicular to the plane of the paper then the force acting on the electron of charge e is given by

$$F = e E$$

This force acts at right angles to the direction of motion of the electron. The electron, therefore, moves along the circular path within the electric field and on leaving the field flies off tangentially to the path meeting the screen at M_1 or M_2 depending upon the direction of the electric field as shown in Fig 7.2 (a) and (b). When a magnetic field B is applied in the plane of the paper perpendicular to the direction of the beam as shown in Fig. 7.3 (a) then according to Fleming's left hand rule the beam is deflected upward out of the paper in a direction perpendicular to both, the direction of motion of the electron and that of the field.

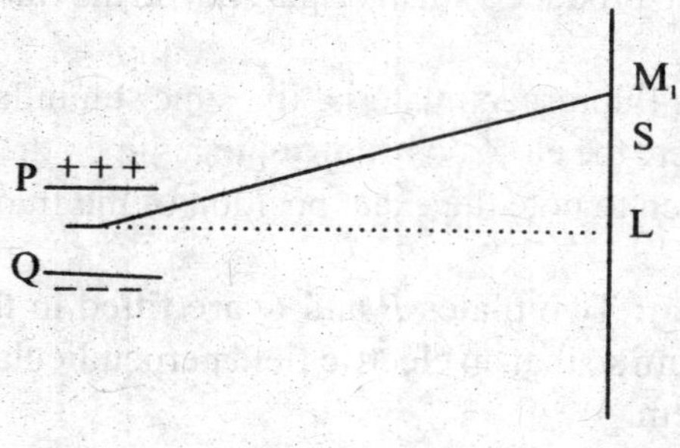

(a)

Fig. 7.2 (a)

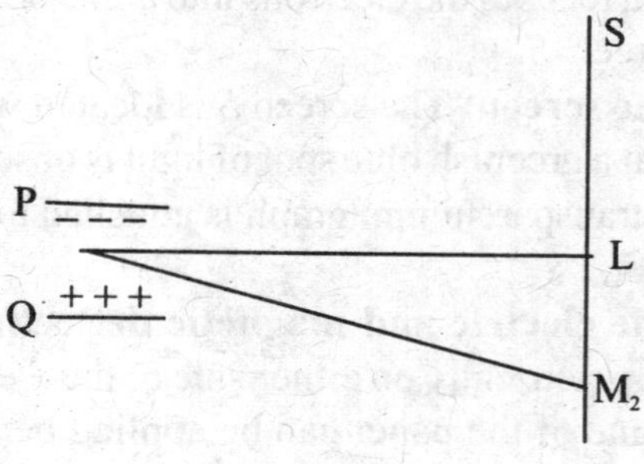

(b)

Fig. 7.2 (b)

When the magnetic field is applied as shown in Fig. 7.3(b), the electron beam is deflected, downward into the paper. If v is the velocity of the electrons in the beam, then magnitude of the force acting on each electron = Bev. As this force also acts at right angles to the direction of motion of the electron, the electron moves along a circular path in the magnetic field and on leaving the field flies off tangentially meeting the screen at M_1 or M_2 as explained above.

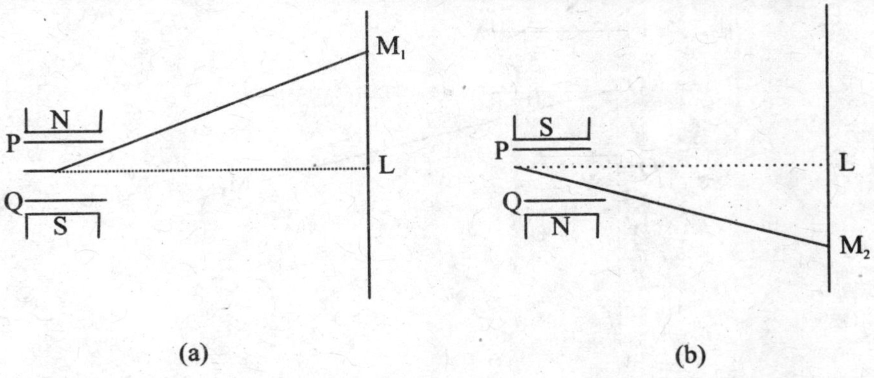

Fig. 7.3(a) **Fig. 7.3(b)**

If *r* is the radius of the circular path along which the electron moves in the magnetic field, then

$$Bev = \frac{mv^2}{r}$$

or $$\frac{e}{m} = \frac{v}{rB} \qquad ...(7.1)$$

To find the velocity of electron *v*: To find the value of v, one of the fields, say the magnetic field is first applied. The spot of light moves from its initial position to the position say M_1. The electric field is now applied simultaneously so as to produce deflection of the electron beam in the opposite direction. The value of the electric field is so adjusted that the spot of light comes back to its initial position. In such a case the forces acting on the electron due to the electric and magnetic fields are equal and opposite.

Therefore, $eE = Bev$

or $$v = \frac{E}{B}$$

Substituting in (7.1), we obtain

$$\frac{e}{m} = \frac{E}{rB^2} \qquad ...(7.2)$$

To find the radius r of circular path: To find the value of *r*, the radius of the circular path in the magnetic field, note the position of the luminous spot on the screen when no field is applied and again when a field *B* is applied. Let the deflection of the spot by $y = LM_2$ a shown. The circular path of the beam *OR* in the magnetic field is as shown in Fig. 7.4. The beam leaves the magnetic field at *R* tangentially to the path and meets the screen at M_2 so that M_2R produced meets *OX* in *T*. Draw *OC* and *RC* perpendiculars to O_1 and RM_2 respectively meeting at *C*, then *C* is the centre of the circular arc *OR* and *OC* = *CR* = radius of the circle = *r*.

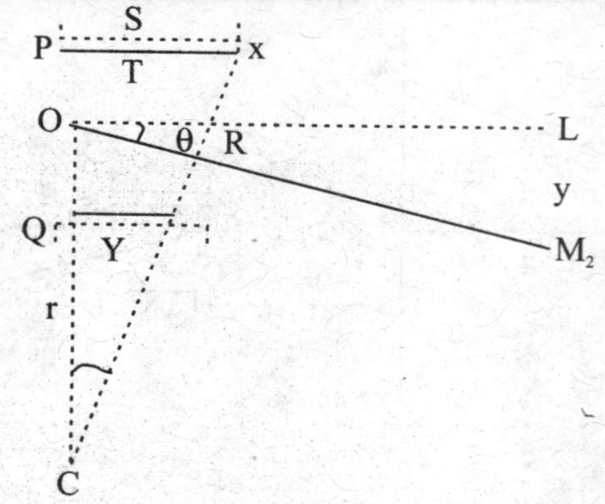

Fig. 7.4

Now $\angle OCR = \angle LTM_2 = \theta$

Therefore $\tan\theta = \dfrac{LM_2}{LT} = \dfrac{OX}{OC}$

or $$r = OC = \frac{LT \times OX}{LM_2}$$

Now *OX* is very nearly equal to the length of the region in which the magnetic field is applied. This is equal to the length of the region in which the electric field is applied i.e., the length of the plates *P* and *Q*. Let it be equal to *l* (This is generally given by the manufacturers).

LT is the distance of the centre of the screen from the centre of the region of the magnetic field (or electric field). Let it be equal to *L*.

Therefore $$r = \frac{lL}{y}$$

Substituting in (7.2), we obtain

$$\frac{e}{m} = \frac{yE}{lLB^2} \quad \text{...(7.3)}$$

The electric field $E = V/d$ where *V* is the potential difference applied between the plates *P* and *Q*. and *d* the distance between the plates (*d* is also given by makers). Substituting in (7.3), we obtain

$$\frac{e}{m} = \frac{yV}{lLdB^2}$$

When *V* is in volts, *B* in tesla and *y*, *l*, and *L* in meters, *e*/*m* is in Coulomb/kg.

WORKING FORMULA

Specific charge of an electron is given by

$$\frac{e}{m}=\frac{yV}{lLdB^2}\times 10^7 \text{ e.m.u./gm}$$

where l is the length of deflection plate, L is the distance of screen from edges of plates, y is total deflection of spot on the screen, d is the separation between the plates P and Q and B is the intensity of magnetic field.

PROCEDURE

1. Draw the North-South line using a compass needle. Also draw the East-West line. Place the cathode ray tube fitted in the wooden frame with its axis along the North-South line so that the rams of the frame lie along the East-West line.
2. Connect the cathode ray tube to the power supply unit. Switch on the current and wait till a luminous bright spot appears on the screen. Adjust the brightness and focus controls so as to get a sharp bright spot in the middle of the screen. Note the initial position of the spot on the scale fitted on the screen.
3. Now apply a suitable deflecting voltage so that the luminous spot is deflected by about 0.5 to 1.0 cm. Note the deflecting voltage V and the position of the spot. Measure the distance through which the spot has moved and let it be y.
4. Place the bar magnets symmetrically on either side of the cathode ray tube along the arms of the wooden stand on which the tube is fitted such that their opposite poles face each other and their common axis is exactly at right angles to the axis of the cathode ray tube. Adjust the polarity as well as the distance of the magnets so that the luminous spot comes back to its initial position. When the adjustment is perfect note the distance of the poles of the magnet on either side nearer to the cathode ray tube. Let the distances be r_1 and r_2.
5. Remove the bar magnets, switch off the electric field applied to the deflecting plates and again note the initial position of the luminous spot. Reverse the polarity of the potential difference applied to the electric deflecting plates with the help of the reversing switch fitted in the power supply unit thereby reversing the electric field. Again note the final position of the luminous spot and calculate y.

   Again place the bar magnets on the arms of the wooden stand as in the previous step and adjust their polarity as well as the distance so that the spot comes back to its initial position. When the adjustment is perfect again note the distances of the poles of the magnets on the side nearer to the cathode ray tube. Let the distances be r_1' and r_2'. Switch off the power supply.
6. To find the value of the magnetic field B, carefully remove the magnets and the cathode ray tube from the wooden stand. Place the compass box (of a deflection magnetometer or tangent galvanometer) such that its entire centre lies exactly on the point where the common axis of the bar magnets and the axis of the cathode ray tube intersect. Rotate the compass box about its vertical axis so that the pointer lies along the 0-0 line.

Place the magnets exactly in the same position as in step 4 at distances r_1 and r_2. This produces a deflection in the magnetometer compass box and the two ends of the pointer give the deflection. Let the readings be θ_1 and θ_2.

Now place the magnets exactly in the same position as in step 5 at distances r_1' and r_2' and again note the deflections θ_1' and θ_2' from the two ends of the pointer of the compass box. The mean of these four deflections θ_1, θ_2, θ_1' and θ_2' gives the mean position θ. If BH is the horizontal component of earth's magnetic field, then $B = B_H \tan\theta$.

7. Take two more sets of observations by changing the value of V and hence that of the electric field.

OBSERVATIONS

Length of the deflecting plates, P or $Q = l = \ldots$ cm

Distance of the screen from the centre of the plates, $L = \ldots$ cm

Distance between the deflecting plates P and Q, $d = \ldots$ cm

Table 1: Determination of deflection y for different values of voltage V

Sr. No.	Applied Voltage V	DIRECT FIELD							REVERSE FIELD						
		Position of spot			Magnetic pole and Distance				Position of spot			Magnetic pole and Distance			
		Initial (cm)	Final (cm)	Deflection y (cm)	Pole	r_1 (cm)	Pole	r_2 (cm)	Initial (cm)	Final (cm)	Deflection y (cm)	Pole	r_1' (cm)	Pole	r_2' (cm)
1	$V_1=$										$y_1=$				
2	$V_2=$										$y_2=$				
3	$V_3=$										$y_3=$				

Horizontal component of earth's magnetic field $B_H = \ldots$ gauss

Table 2: For determination of B

S. No.	Applied Voltage (volt)	Reading of two ends of pointer when magnetic poles are at r_1 and r_2		Reading of two ends of pointer when magnetic poles are at r_1' and r_2'		Mean θ	$B = B_H \tan\theta$
		θ_1	θ_2	θ_1'	θ_2'		
1	V_1						B_1
2	V_2						B_2
3	V_3						B_3

CALCULATIONS

(i) First set: $\frac{e}{m} = \frac{y_1 V_1}{lLdB_1^{\,2}}$ = ... e.m.u./gm

(ii) Second set: $\frac{e}{m} = \frac{y_2 V_2}{lLdB_2^{\,2}}$ = ... e.m.u./gm.

(iii) Third set: $\frac{e}{m} = \frac{y_3 V_3}{lLdB_3^{\,2}}$ = ... e.m.u./gm.

Mean *e/m* = ... e.m.u./gm

RESULT: e/m for an electron = ... e.m.u./gm.

Standard value of e/m = 1.76×10^7 e.m.u./gm

Therefore, percentage error = ... %.

PRECAUTIONS AND SOURCES OF ERROR

1. The cathode ray tube must be set in the north south direction.
2. The luminous spot on the screen should be sharp, bright and in the middle.
3. The deflecting voltage must produce a deflection of the order of 0.5 to 1.0 cm.
4. The axis of the bar magnets and the axis of the cathode ray tube must be exactly at right angles and in a horizontal plane.
5. The deflecting voltage must be reversed to produce the deflection of the spot of light in the opposite direction and the magnetic field must also be reversed to bring it back to initial position.
6. The cathode ray tube must be handed carefully.

VIVA-VOCE

Q. 1. What is the specific charge of an electron?

Ans. The ratio of charge on an electron to its rest mass is called specific charge. The value of *e/m* is 1.7610^{11} Coulomb/kg.

Q. 2. What is the unit of e/m?

Ans. The S.I. unit of e/m is Coulomb/kg. Other units are e.m.u./gm and e.s.u./gm.

Q. 3. What do you mean by magnetic meridian?

Ans. A magnetic meridian is an imaginary arc on the earth's surface from North Pole to the South Pole that connects all locations running along it with a given longitude.

Q. 4. What is the principle of Thomson's experiment?

Ans. The experiment is based on the principle that an electron beam while passing through an electric or magnetic field obeys the same laws at those observed by a current carrying conductor.

Q. 5. State the formula for e/m in Thomson's method in terms of v and B.

Ans. The specific charge is given by, $\frac{e}{m} = \frac{v}{rB}$ where r is the radius of circular path along which the electrons move in the magnetic field.

Q. 6. What is the relation between the velocity of the electrons, electric field E and magnetic field B when both the fields applied simultaneously produce no deflection?

Ans. The relation is $v = E/B$.

Q. 7. What is the direction of the electric and magnetic field in Thomson's method?

Ans. Ref. to Fig. 1, the electric field between the plates P and Q is perpendicular to the plane of the paper and magnetic field is applied at the same place in a direction perpendicular to the direction of the electric field i.e., in the plane of the paper.

Q. 8. How do you find the radius of the circular trace of the electron beam?

Ans. The radius of circular trace of the electron beam is given by $r = Ll/y$. where l is the length of deflection plate, L is the distance of screen from edges of plates, and y is total deflection of spot on the screen.

❑❑❑

EXPERIMENT 8

AIM

To determine the internal resistance of Leclenche cell with the help of a potentiometer.

APPARATUS

A potentiometer, Leclenche cell, two one way keys, a sensitive galvanometer, rheostat, two resistance boxes, jockey, an ammeter, a voltmeter, connection wires, sand paper etc.

THEORY

Potentiometer is a device used to measure the internal resistance of a cell. It can also be used to measure e.m.f. of a given cell and to compare e.m.f.'s of the cells. It is based on the principle of Wheatstone bridge. It consists of a long resistive wire of length about 3 to 10 m long made up of mangnine or constantan and a battery of known voltage E and internal resistance r called supplier battery or deliver cell. The experimental arrangement is shown in Fig. 8.1.

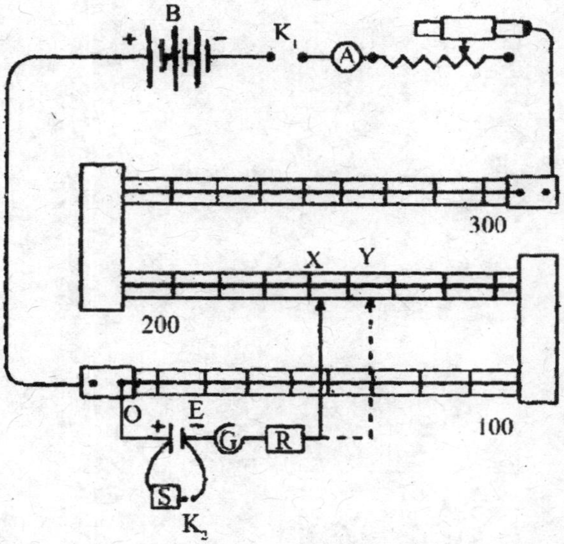

Fig.8.1 Experimental arrangement

Let the potential difference across the terminals of the cell when no current is drawn from it be E and the potential difference when it sends a current to the resistance S be V, then we have

$$r = \frac{E - V}{V} \times S \qquad \text{... (8.1)}$$

The values of E and V are determined in terms of length of the potentiometer wire.

Let l_1 is the length of the wire to the point where a balance point is obtained in an open circuit, then

$$E = \rho I l_1. \qquad \text{.. (8.2)}$$

where ρ is the resistance per cm. length of the wire and I is the current flowing through the wire.

Let the balance point is obtained at l_2 when the cell passes a current through the resistance S, then

$$V = \rho I l_2. \qquad \text{....(8.3)}$$

Therefore, from equation (8.1), we obtain

$$r = \frac{l_1 - l_2}{l_2} \times S.$$

Knowing the values of l_1, l_2, and S, we can determine the internal resistance of the cell.

PROCEDURE

1. Draw diagram showing the scheme of connections Fig. 8.1 and make the connections accordingly. Take out 5000 ohm resistance from the resistance box.
2. To test the connections, introduce the plug in the key K_1 and keep K_2 open. Press the jockey at the zero end and note the direction of deflection. Now put the jockey at the other end, if the direction of deflection is opposite to that in the first case, the connections are correct. If the direction of deflection is the same, then increase the current in the main circuit till the deflection in the second case is reversed.
3. Move the jockey along the wire to find a point where the galvanometer gives zero. Insert the 5000 ohms plug and find the null point accurately as at X. Note that length l_1 of the wire and the current in the ammeter. Put the key K_2 and take out 1 ohm plug from the resistance box S and make all other plugs tight. Find the balance point again as at Y and note the corresponding length l_2. Repeat twice for the same value of the current in the auxiliary circuit and same shunt resistance in a similar manner to avoid any error.
4. Put the plugs from the keys K_1 and K_2. Wait for some time, put the plug in the key K_1 and find l_1 keeping the current same in a similar manner. Put the plug in the key K_2, take out a resistance of 2, 3, 4 ohms and find the length l_1 in each case.
5. Take similar readings by varying the current in the main circuit.

OBSERVATIONS

Table 1: Determination of internal resistance *r*

Sr. No.	Ammeter reading (ampere)	Position of null point						Shunt resistance S (ohm)	Internal resistance $\frac{l_1 - l_2}{l_2} \times S$ (ohm)
		without shunt			with shunt				
		(a) (cm)	(b) (cm)	Mean l_1 (cm)	(a) (cm)	(b) (cm)	Mean l_2 (cm)		
1 2 3									
1 2 3									

CALCULATIONS

Mean value of resistance of the cell from observations = ... ohm.

RESULT

Internal resistance of the cell = ... ohm.

PRECAUTIONS AND SOURCES OF ERROR

1. The e.m.f. of the auxiliary battery should be constant and always more than the e.m.f. of the cell, whose internal resistance is to be found out.
2. The positive pole of the battery and the positive pole of the cell must be connected to the terminal on the zero side of the potentiometer wire.
3. The rheostat should be of a low resistance and the current must be changed to get the null point at a desired length.
4. The current should remain constant for each set of readings.
5. The current should be passed only for the duration it is necessary, otherwise the balance point will go vary.
6. The internal resistance of a Leclanche cell is not constant but increases with the current drawn from the cell. So to get concordant readings the resistance from the resistance box *S* must be changed by a small amount.

VIVA-VOCE

Q. 1. What do you mean by the internal resistance of a cell?

Ans. When a cell is connected in the circuit, current flows from negative pole to the positive pole inside the electrolyte. The resistance offered by the electrolyte to the flow of current is called internal resistance of the cell.

Q. 2. Is the internal resistance a constant quantity for the cell?

Ans. No, it changes with the strength of the current drawn, i.e. if the current drawn is high, more will be the internal resistance of the cell.

Q. 3. What is a potentiometer? What is its principle?

Ans. A potentiometer is a device used to measure e.m.f. of a given cell, compare e.m.f.'s of the cells, and to measure internal resistance of a cell. It is based on the principle of Wheatstone bridge.

Q. 4. What is Wheatstone bridge?

Ans. It is an arrangement to measure an unknown electrical resistance by balancing two legs of a bridge circuit, one leg of which includes the unknown component.

Q. 5. What is the basic principle of your method of finding the internal resistance of the cell?

Ans. When we draw the current from a cell, e.m.f. drops due to internal resistance of the cell. From potentiometer readings, l_1 and l_2 balance E and V and $E/V = l_1/l_2$.

Q. 6. Name some other methods for finding the internal resistance of a cell.

Ans. Mance's method, which gives more accurate result.

Q. 7. Which cell do you use for finding the internal resistance of a cell?

Ans. Leclanche cell.

Q. 8. Why don't you use a secondary cell for this purpose?

Ans. The secondary cells are rechargeable. They have very low internal resistance and hence they are not used for this purpose.

Q. 9. Why we do not disturb the cell whose internal resistance is being measured during the experiment?

Ans. The internal resistance will change with disturbance.

Q. 10. Why do you get null point in the second case at a shorter length of wire?

Ans. In first case, cell is open circuit and its e.m.f. is balanced but in second case e.m.f. falls due to internal resistance of the cell and so balancing length becomes less.

Q.11. Why do you use a high resistance in series with the galvanometer?

Ans. This is preferably because the current drawn from the cell, at the time of locating null point, will be small and so internal resistance may not change during the observations. However it will make galvanometer insensitive.

Q.12. What is the difference between e.m.f. and the potential difference?

Ans. The e.m.f. is the maximum voltage across the terminals of the cell when no current is drawn from the cell while potential difference is the voltage across the terminals of the cell when current is drawn from it.

□□□

EXPERMENT 9

AIM

To determine the resistance per unit length of a Carey Foster's bridge wire and also to find out the specific resistance of a given wire.

APPARATUS

Carey Foster's bridge, Leclanche cell, galvanometer, a rheostat of low resistance (or two one ohm coils), decimal resistance box, copper strip, a key, a resistance of know length.

THEORY

Carey Foster's bridge is based on the principle of Wheat stone's bridge and it is an improved form of meter bridge. In this bridge the sensitivity is increased by dividing the resistance wire of one metre in two parts by jockey and extra resitances connected in series with these parts of wire.

Carey Foster's bridge consists of a resistance wire of 1 metre length and of uniform cross–section fixed on a wooden board. Terminals are fixed at the gaps. Almost equal resistances P and Q (in general 1ohm standard coils) are connected in the inner two gaps. In the outer two gaps known and unknown resistance X and Y respectively are connected. A leclanche cell with key is connected between the strips A and C and a galvanometer G is connected between the strip B the jockey D, as shown in figure 9.1

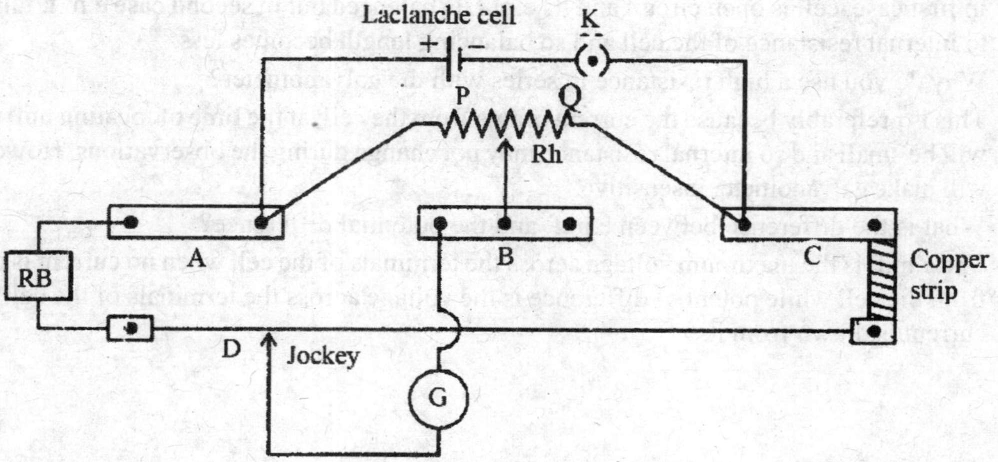

Fig. 9.1 Carey Foster's bridge

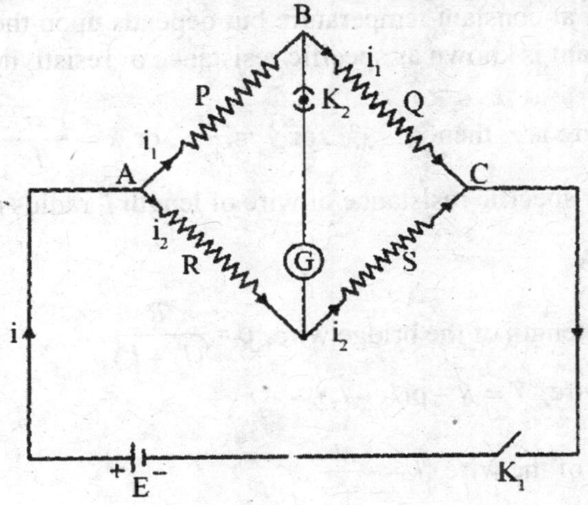

Fig. 9.2 Wheatstone bridge

According to Wheatstone's bridge principle, when the potentials at points B and D are same i.e. bridge containing four arms P, Q, R and S is balanced, then the deflection in the galvanometer is zero and the balancing condition is given by $\frac{P}{Q}=\frac{R}{S}$.

Determination of ρ : The resistance per unit length of Carey Foster's bridge wire is given by

$$\rho = \frac{R_1}{(l_2 - l_1)} \quad \text{....(9.1)}$$

Determination of unknown resistance *Y*: For the determination of unknown resistance (say *Y*) connect it in gap Y and connect the resistance box R in gap X. Let the balancing length obtained is l_3 and on interchanging X and Y the balancing length obtained is l_4, then

$$Y = R - \rho\,(l_4 - l_3) \quad \text{...(9.2)}$$

Using equation (9.1), we obtain

$$Y = R - \frac{(l_4 - l_3)R_1}{(l_2 - l_1)}$$

From this equation the unknown resistance Y can be determined.

Specific resistance. From experiments it is observed that at constant temperature, the resistance Y of a resistance wire is

(i) directly proportional to the length l of the wire and

(ii) inversely proportional to the cross–sectional area A of the wire.

Thus $\quad Y \alpha \frac{l}{A}$ or $Y = k\frac{l}{A}$

where k is a constant at constant temperature but depends upon the nature f the material of resistance wire. This constant is known as specific resistance or resistivity of the wire.

If the radius of the wire is r, then $A = \pi r^2$, or $Y = \frac{kl}{\pi r^2}$, or $k = \frac{Y\pi r^2}{l}$

This is expression for specific resistance of wire of length l, radius r and resistance Y.

WORKING FORMULA

(i) The resistance per unit length of the bridge wire, $\rho = \frac{R}{(l_2 - l_1)}$.

(ii) The resistance of the wire, $Y = R - \rho(l_4 - l_3)$.

(iii) The specific resistance of the wire, $k = \frac{Y\pi r^2}{l}$.

PROCEDURE

Determination of ρ

1. Make the connection as shown in figure 9.1.
2. Adjust the sliding contact of the rheostat in the middle.
3. Introduce a low resistance (say 0.1 Ω) from deciohm box and close key *k*.
4. Determine the position of null point by sliding the jockey on the bridge wire.
5. Note the position of this null point from the left end of the bridge.
6. Repeat this process by introducing two or three resistance.
7. Now mutually exchange the position of the deciohm box and the copper strip. Again determine the balancing lengths for the same values of resistance introduced in the deciohm box.
8. Note down the position of null points from the same left end of the bridge.
9. Calculate ρ for each set and then determine mean ρ.

Determination of unknown resistance *Y*

1. Take a resisance wire whose specific resistance is to be determined and replace it with the coper strip as shown in figure 9.1, other connections remains same.
2. Follow the procedure as explain above.
3. Note down the position of null points.
4. Calculate unknown resistance *Y* for each set and then determine mean *Y*.

OBSERVATIONS

Table 1: Determination of ρ

S. No.	Resistance introduced in resistance box (Ω)	Position of null point when resistance R is		$(l_2 - l_1)$ cm	$\rho = R/(l_2 - l_1)$ Ω/cm
		In left gap l_1 (cm)	In right gap l_2 (cm)		
1.					
2.					
3.					

Mean ρ = ...Ω/cm

Table 2: Determination of unknown resistance *Y*

S. No.	Resistance introduced in resistance box R (Ω)	Position of null point when resistance R is		$(l_4 - l_3)$ cm	$Y=R-\rho(l_4-l_3)$ (Ω)
		In left gap l_3 (cm)	In right gap l_4 (cm)		
1.					
2.					
3.					

Mean Y = ...Ω

Length of wire, l = ...cm

Radius of wire, r = ...cm

CALCULATION

(i) The resistance per unit length of the bridge wire, $\rho = \dfrac{R}{(l_2 - l_1)}$ = ... ohm/cm.

(ii) The resistance of the wire, $Y = R - \rho(l_4 - l_3)$ = ... ohm.

(iii) The specific resistance of the wire, $k = \dfrac{Y\pi r^2}{l}$ =....ohm-cm.

RESULT

Specific resistance of the material of a wire k = ...ohm–cm

Standard value (Manganin) $k = 42\times10^{-6}$ ohm–cm.

Percentage error = ...%.

PRECAUTIONS AND SOURCES OF ERROR

1. The key K used in the bridge must be closed only when observations are taken otherwise unnecessary current flowing in the bridge wire will be heat it up and this will change the resistance per unit length of the wire.
2. The resistance of the rheostat must be low.
3. The jockey must be pressed gently and momentarily on the wire and it should not be slided in contact with the wire. Due to this the wire becomes non-uniform.

VIVA–VOCE

Q.1 What is specific resistance?

Ans. The specific resistance (k), or resistivity of a material is the resistance offered by a wire of this material which is one cm long with a cross sectional area of 1 cm^2. It is the resistance in ohms offered by a unit volume of a substance of the flow of electric current. It is a property of any conductive material.

Q.2 Has temperature any effect on the specific resistance ?

Ans. Yes, the specific resistance of pure metals decreases with increasing temperature.

Q.3 What is the material of the Carey Foster's bridge wire ?

Ans. The bridge wire is of manganin or constantan.

Q.4 Why should the jockey be not pressed too hard ?

Ans. If jockey is pressed too hard, the wire will become flat at that point and its area of cross–section will no longer be uniform and hence the resistance of the wire will not be proportional to its length.

Q.5 What is the minimum and maximum difference in resistance that you can measure with Carey Foster's bridge wire?

Ans. Minimum difference measured by this bridge wire is resistance of one millimeter length to the bridge wire. Maximum difference is equal to the resistance of the total length of the bridge wire.

Q.6 What is the relation between resistivity and conductivity ?

Ans. Restivity is the reciprocal of conductivity. Any substance that has a high resistivity will have a low conductivity, and vice versa.

Q.7 What do you mean by end correction ?

Ans. Since the Carey Fosters bridge wire is soldered at its end with thick copper strips. If the soldering is not perfect it may give resistance, the way to eliminate this resistance is known as end correction.

❑❑❑

EXPERMENT 10

AIM

To plot graph showing the variation of magnetic field with distance along the axis of a circular coil carrying current and hence estimate the radius of the coil.

APPARATUS

An accumulator, a rheostat, an ammeter, a plug key, a commutator and Stewart and Gee's tangent galvanometer.

THEORY

To study the variation of magnetic field along the axis of a circular coil Stewart and Gee's type of tangent galvanometer, as shown in Fig. 10.1, is used. It consists of a circular wooden or brass frame on which are wound a number of turns of insulated copper wire. The coil is fixed on a horizontal base with its plane vertical and the free ends of the wire are connected to two terminals T_1 and T_2 provided at the base. A deflection galvanometer is fitted on the two pillars provided on the horizontal board in such a manner that it can slide along the horizontal direction with the centre of the needle always lying on the axis of the coil. The distance of the needle from the centre of the coil can be read on the centimeter scale provided on the magnetometer arms with reference to fixed marks on the vertical pillars.

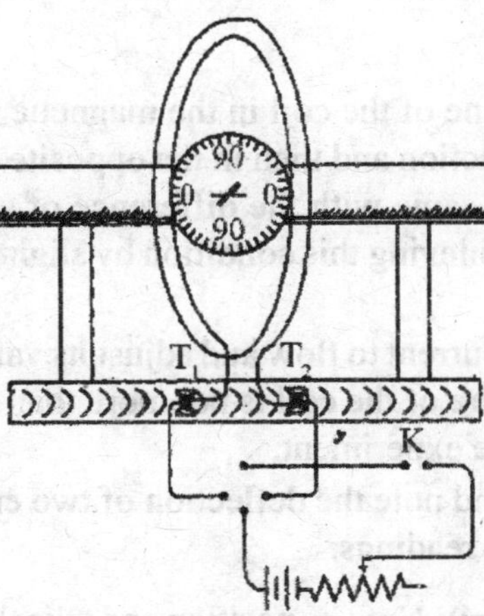

Fig. 10.1 Stewart and Gee's tangent galvanometer

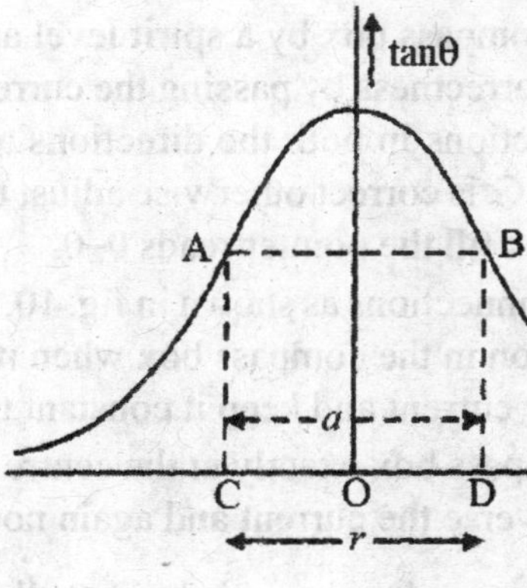

Fig. 10.2 Variation of magnetic field

The magnetic field density B at a distance r on the axis of current carring coil is

$$B = \frac{\mu_0 n I a^2}{2(a^2 + r^2)^{3/2}} \quad ...10.1$$

where, μ_0 is permability of free space ($4\pi \times 10^{-7}$ H/m), n is number of turns in coil, I is current in coil (amp.) and a is radius of coil (cm).

Also, by tangent law

$$B = B_H \tan\theta \quad ....10.2$$

where B_H is horizontal component of earth's magnetic field and θ is deflection in magnetometer

Thus, $B \,\alpha \tan\theta$, so a graph is plotted between $\tan\theta$ and r from equation (i) and (ii), and also,

$$(\tan\theta)_r = \pm\frac{a}{2} = 0.715(\tan\theta)_{r=0}$$

using this equation we can determine radius of coil.

WORKING FORMULA

If the external magnetic field is made perpedicular to the horizontal component of earth's magnetic field, than the deflection of the magnetometer needle is given by $B = B_H \tan\theta$.

Hence a graph between the axial distance r and $\tan\theta$ is plotted. The points of inflexion are identified from both sides of the curve (Fig. 10.2). The distance between the two points is the radius of circular coil.

PROCEDURE

1. Level the compass box by a spirit level and set the plane of the coil in the magnetic meridian. Check its correctness by passing the current in one direction and then in the opposite direction. If the deflections in both the directions are nearly the same with the difference of say 2°, the setting of T.G. is correct otherwise adjust the coil for achieving this condition by slight. Turn the compass box till the pointer reads 0–0.
2. Make the connections as shown in fig. 10.1. Allow the current to flow and adjust its value so that the deflection in the compass box when it is at the centre of the coil is not more than 80°. Note the value of current and keep it constant throughout the experiment.
3. Set the compass box exactly at the centre of this coil and note the deflection of two ends of the pointer. Reverse the current and again note the pointer readings.
4. Shift the compass box one side by a small distance (~ 5cm). Note its position and take the radings of the pointer with direct and the reverse current.
5. Take a number of such sets of observations at varous positions of the compass box, on the axis of the coil, by displacing it in steps of 5 cm initially and then by 1 cm where the variation becomes too rapid.

6. Repeat the whole procedure on the other side of the coil.
7. Find mean θ and tan θ for each set of observation and plot a smooth graph between tan θ and *r*, the distance from the centre of the coil.
8. Find the positions of the points of inflection on the two branches of the curve. The distance between these positions gives the radius of the coil.
9. Find the maximum value of tan θ and calculate the value of tan θ and calculate the value of 0.715 B_{max} or 0.715 $(\tan\theta)_{max}$. Determine the position on the curve where $\tan\theta = 0.715 \tan\theta_{max}$. This positions in cm also gives the radius of the coil.

OBSERVATIONS

Current flowing through the coil *I* = ...Amp.

Number of turns in coil *n* = ...

Table 1: Determination of tan θ

S.No.	*Distance of the needle along the axis from the centre of coil r (cm)*	*Compass box on left hand side Deflection in degrees*						*Compass box on right hand side Deflection in degrees*					
		Direct current		*Reverse current*		*Mean* θ	*tan* θ	*Direct current*		*Reverse current*		*Mean* θ	*tan* θ
		θ_1	θ_2	θ_3	θ_4			θ_1	θ_2	θ_3	θ_4		
1.													
2.													
3.													
4.													
5.													
6.													
7.													
8.													

CALCULATIONS

1. The radius of the coil is calcualted by dropping perpendiculars from the points of inflection *A* and *B* on two branches of the curve so as to meet the *r*–axis at *C* and *D*. The distance between *C* and *D* = *a*, the radius of the coil.
2. Calculate the radius of the coil by the second method also by measuring $(\tan\theta)_{max}$ on the graph and choosing a point on the y–axis such that $\tan\theta = 0.715(\tan\theta)_{max}$. The *r*–coordinate of this point gives the radius of the coil.

RESULT

1. The variation of tan θ and hence that of field *B* with distance *r* from the centre of the coil is as shown in the attached graph.
2. The radius of the given coil = ...cm.

PRECAUTIONS AND SOURCE OF ERROR

1. The plane of the coil should be set exactly in the magnetic meridian.
2. No magnetic material or current carrying wire should lie in the vicinity of this apparatus.
3. Both the ends of the aluminium pointer should be read.
4. Deflection should be recorded by passing direct as well as reverse current.
5. The current should be such that the deflecting at the centre may not exceed 70° at the most.
6. The point of inflexion should be correctly noted.
7. Reading should be taken only after tapping the top of the glass cover as sometimes it gets stuck.
8. Throughout the experiment the current should remain constant.

VIVA-VOCE

Q.1 What is the direction of the magnetic field at the centre of this coil?

Ans. The direction of the magnetic field at the centre of the coil is normal to its plane.

Q.2 In the study of this experiment, where do you expect the magnetic field to be maximum?

Ans. The field due to the current is maximum at the centre of the coil.

Q.3 Is there any special property of the field near the centre ?

Ans. Yes. The peculiarity of the field near the centre is that it is uniform, i.e. the lines of force due to the current in a small region round about the centre are equidistant and parallel.

Q.4 What do you mean by tangent law?

Ans. If two uniform mutually perpendicualr fields (B and B_0) act on a small magnet, then in equilibrium the ratio of two fields is equal to $\tan\theta$.

Q.5 What do you mean by magnetic meridian ?

Ans. It is an imaginary vertical plane passing through the magnetic axis (N–S pole line) of a freely suspended magnet.

Q.6 How do you ascertain that the coil is in magnetic meridian ?

Ans. By reversing current through the coil. If the deflection due to direct and reverse currents are identical, then coil is set in magnetic meridian.

Q.7 What do you mean by the point of inflection ?

Ans. The point where the curve changes its curvature.

Q.8 What is magnetic induction ?

Ans. The number of magnetic lines of force passing through unit normal area at any point in a magnetic field is defined as magnetic induction at the point.

Q.9 How does the magnetic field vary along the axis of the coil ?

Ans. If the field strength (B) is plotted against the distance (r) from the centre of the coil, the curve is first concave towards the origin. At a distance equal to half the radius, the curvature changes sign and then the curve becomes convex towards the origin (Fig. 10.2)

Q. 10 What is S.I. unit of magnetic induction?

Ans. It is Weber/meter^2 or Tesla or Newton/Amp. meter.

Q. 11 State Ampere's law ?

Ans. The line integral of magnetic induction along any closed path in a magnetic field is equal to the product of μ_0 and the total net current enclosed by that closed path, i.e.

$$\oint_c \vec{B}.\vec{d\ell} = \mu_0 \sum i$$

Q. 12 What is magnetomotive force ?

Ans. The line integral of magnetising force along any closed path in a magnetic field is defined as the magnetomotive force.

$$MMF = \oint_c \vec{H}.\vec{d\ell}$$

Q. 13 What is the unit of magnetomotive force ?

Ans. Its unit is Anpere.

Q. 14 How does current carrying small coil behave ?

Ans. Current caryingsmall coil behaves like a small magnetic dipole.

Q. 15 If it behaves like a magnetic dipole, then what is its magnetic moment?

Ans. The mapetic moment of a small current carrying coil is equal to the product of the current flowingn the coil and the effective area of coil.

□□□

EXPERIMENT 11

AIM

To determine the value of acceleration due to gravity in the laboratory using bar pendulum.

APPARATUS

Bar pendulum, knife edges, stop watch, metre scale.

THEORY

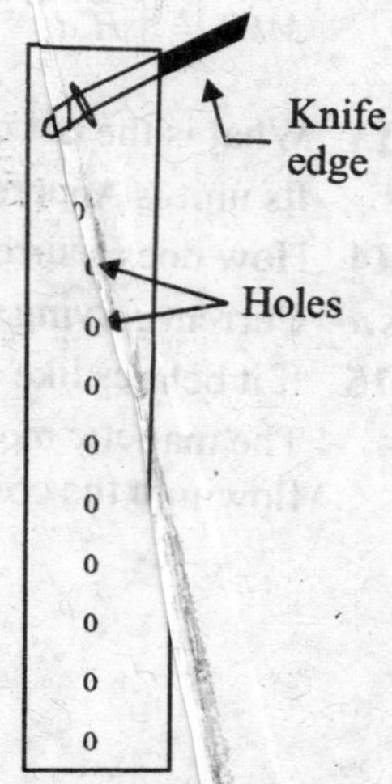

Fig. 11.1 Bar endulum

A bar pendulum is a meter long uniform rectangular bar consists of holes in a straight line along its length at equal distances from each other as shown in Fig. 11.1. This is also known as compound pendulum, physical pendulum or a rigid pendulum.

The point in which the vertical plane (knife edge) passing through CG of the pendulum meets the axis of rotation is called its centre of suspension and the distance between the point of suspension and the CG of the pendulum measures the length of the pendulum.

In this case $T=2\sqrt{\frac{I}{mgl}}$ (I is moment of inertia)

$I = I_0 + ml^2$ (I_0 is moment of inertia of the pendulum about an axis throught its C.G. parallel to the axis)

$$= mK^2 + ml^2$$

$$= m\left(K^2 + l^2\right)$$

$$\therefore \quad T = 2\pi\sqrt{\frac{m\left(K^2 + l^2\right)}{mgl}} = 2\pi\sqrt{\frac{K^2 + l^2}{gl}} = 2\pi\sqrt{\frac{K^2/l + l}{g}}$$

$$\therefore \quad T = 2\pi\sqrt{\frac{\frac{K^2}{l} + l}{g}} \text{ or } g = \frac{4\pi^2\left(\frac{K^2}{l} l\right)}{T^2}$$

WORKING FORMULA

As the bar pendulum will execute simple harmonic motion for one hole then time period

$$T = 2\pi\sqrt{\frac{L}{g}}$$

or acceleration due to gravity $g = \frac{4\pi^2 L}{T^2}$ m/sec^2

where L is distance between centres of oscillation and suspension (measured using the graph of time period T versus distance of hole from one end) as shown in Fig. 11.2.

PROCEDURE

1. The bar pendulum is hung vertically by means of a sharp knife edge.
2. Now oscillate the bar pendulum with knife edge passing through the first hole and note down the time taken for bar pendulum to oscillate 20 oscillations (by using stop watch).
3. Hence Time period $T = \frac{\text{Number of oscillations (20)}}{\text{time taken}}$
4. Insert the knife edge in the second hole and find the time period and continue to do so for subsequent holes till the centre of gravity is reched.
5. Turn the bar pendulum and repeat the same procedure.
6. Plot a graph between time period T and the distance of sharp knife edge x taking origin in the centre of the graph.

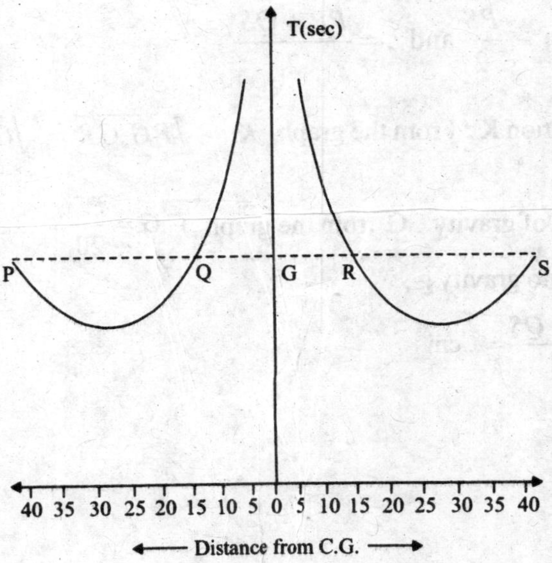

Fig. 11.2 Time period versus distance from C.G.

OBSERAVATIONS

Table 1: Determination of time period (T)

No. of holes	*Distance of the hole from one end of the bar l (cm)*	*No. of oscillations*	*Time Taken (sec)*	*Time Period T (sec)*
1		20		
2		20		
3		20		
:		:		
:		:		
9.		20		
C.G.				
10.		20		
11.		20		
:				

CALCULATIONS

Plot a graph between time period T versus l. At a particular time period T_1 draw a horizontal line giving four points of intersection with the curve (as shown in Fig. 11.2).

From graph $PR = QS = l + \frac{K^2}{l} = L$

Centre of gravity C.G. = $\frac{PS}{2}$ and $L = \frac{PR + QS}{2}$

(i) The radius of gyration K : From the graph, $K = \sqrt{PG.GR} = \sqrt{GS.QG} = ...\text{cm}$

(ii) Position of centre of gravity CG, from the graph, $C.G = \frac{PS}{20} = ...\text{cm}$

(iii) Acceleration due to gravity g :

From graph $L = \frac{PR + QS}{2} = ...\text{cm}$

$T = ...$ sec

$g = \frac{4\pi^2 L}{T^2} = ...\text{cm/s}^2$

RSESULT

Radius of gyration K = ... cm

Centre of gravity C.G. = ...

Accceleration due to gravity g = ... cm/sec² at .... (Name of city where expt. is performed) standard value of g (from the Table at the end of book) at ... (Name of city) is .... cm/sec².

$$\therefore \quad \text{percentage} = \frac{\text{Standard value - Observed value}}{\text{Standard value}} \times 100\%$$

$$= ....\%$$

PRECAUTIONS

1. Knife edge must be horizontal.
2. Holes in the bar pendulum must be identical.
3. The amplitude of oscillation should be kept small.
4. Graphs should be smooth.

VIVA-VOCE

Q.1 What is bar pendulum ?

Ans. A bar pendulum is a meter long uniform rectangular bar consists of holes in a straight line along its length of equal distances from each other.

Q.2. What are the other names of bar pendulum.

Ans. Bar pendulum is also known as compound pendulum, physical pendulum or rigid pendulum.

Q.3. What is meant by centre of suspension.

Ans. Centre of suspension is the point at which the vertical plane (knife edge) passing through centre of gravity (C.G) of the pendulum meets the axits of rotation.

Q.4. How does the period vary with distance of knife edge from C.G. of the pendulum ?

Ans. At C.G. time period is infinite and after that the time period decreases rapidly and becomes minimum when the distance is equal to radius of gyration. Then again the period starts increasing at greater distances.

Q.5. What is the length of equivalent simple pendulum ?

Ans. For bar pendulum time period

$$T = 2\pi\sqrt{\frac{(K^2/l + l)}{g}} = 2\pi\sqrt{\frac{L}{g}}$$

where $L = \sqrt{(K^2/l + l)}$

This is known as the length of equivalent simple pendulum.

Q.6. A uniform circular disc of radius R oscillates in a vertical plane about a horizontal axis. Find the distance of the axis of rotation from the centre for which the period is minimum. What is the value of this period ?

Ans. The circular disc oscillates as a compound pendulum of length l, whose time-period is $T = 2\pi\sqrt{\frac{(K^2/l + l)}{g}}$ where K its radius of gyration about an axis through its centre of gravity. As we know, that the time-period of a compound pendulum is minimum when its length is equal to its radius of gyration about its C.G. i.e. when $l = K$.

$$T_{min} = 2\pi\sqrt{\frac{(K^2/K + K)}{g}} = 2\pi\sqrt{\frac{K}{g}}$$

Since the moment of inertia of a disc about an axis perpendicular to its plane and passing through its centre is : $I = MK^2 = \frac{1}{2}MR^2$ where M is the mass of the disc and R, its radius,

we have $K^2 = \frac{R^2}{2}$

$$\therefore \quad K = \frac{R}{\sqrt{2}}$$

$$\therefore \quad T_{min} = 2\pi\sqrt{\frac{\sqrt{2}}{g}} = 2\pi\sqrt{\frac{\sqrt{2}R}{g}}$$

❏❏❏

EXPERIMENT 12

AIM

To determine the moment of inertia of a flywheel about its own axis of rotation.

APPARATUS

A flywheel, a few different masses and a mass provided with a hook, a strong and thin string, stop watch, a meter rod, a vernier calipers and a piece of chalk.

THEORY

A flywheel is simply a heavy wheel with a long axle supported in bearings such that it can rest in any position. In other words the centre of gravity lies on the axis of rotation.

To find the moment of inertia of a flywheel, a mass *m* is attached to the axle of the flywheel by a chord which is wrapped several times round the axle. One end of the string is in the form of a loop so that it can easily be attached to or detached from a pin projecting from the axle. The length of the string is so adjusted that it gets detached from the axle as soon as the bottom of the mass *m* is just to touch the floor. The experimental arrangement is shown in Fig. 12.1.

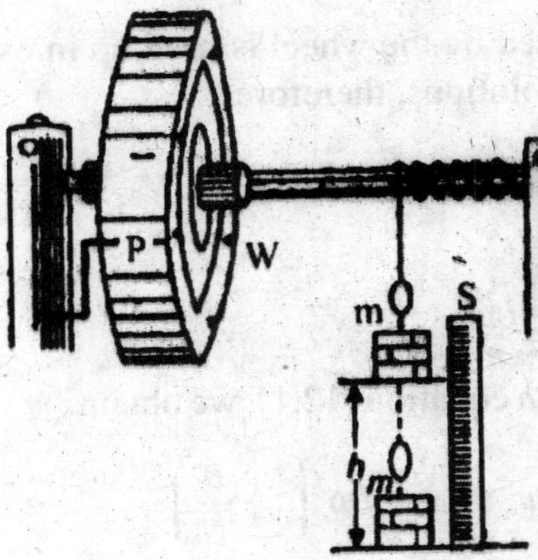

Fig. 12.1 Experimental arrangement

When the mass is allowed to fall, its potential energy is partly converted into the kinetic energy due to the velocity gained by it and partly into the energy of rotation of the flywheel.

Let ω be the angular velocity imparted to the flywheel at the moment the mass *m* is detached.

After the string has been detached from the wheel, the wheel continues to revolve for some time. Its angular velocity decreases on account of friction and finally the wheel comes to rest. If *N* is the number of revolutions that the wheel makes in time *t* before coming to rest, then

Average angular velocity $= \dfrac{2\pi N}{t}$.

If the frictional force is constant the motion of the wheel is uniformly retarded. It begins with an angular velocity ω and its final angular velocity is zero, so that the initial velocity ω is double the average velocity.

or $$\omega = 2 \times \frac{2\pi N}{t} = \frac{4\pi N}{t}.$$

According to the law of conservation of energy, when the string is detached,

P.E. of mass m = K.E. of mass m + K.E. of wheel + Work done against friction.

If h is the height through which the mass has fallen, then

P.E. of mass $m = mgh$

If r is the radius of the axle, then

Linear velocity of mass $m = r\omega$

K.E. of mass $m = \frac{1}{2}m(r\omega)^2$.

If I is the moment of inertia of the flywheel, then its K.E. $= \frac{1}{2}I\omega^2$

Let F be the energy per revolution used in overcoming the frictional force. If n is the number of revolutions the wheel makes during the descent of the mass m, then

Total energy used to overcome friction = nF.

Hence, $$mgh = \frac{1}{2}mr^2\omega^2 + \frac{1}{2}I\omega^2 + nF \qquad ....(12.1)$$

The kinetic energy possessed by the wheel is used up in overcoming friction. As the wheel comes to rest after making N revolutions, therefore

$$NF = \frac{1}{2}I\omega^2$$

or $$F = \frac{1}{N}\frac{1}{2}I\omega^2$$

Substituting the value of F in equation (12.1), we obtain

$$mgh = \frac{1}{2}mr^2\omega^2 + \frac{1}{2}I\omega^2\left(1 + \frac{n}{N}\right)$$

or $$I = \frac{2mgh - mr^2\omega^2}{\omega^2(1+n/N)} \qquad ....(12.2)$$

WORKING FORMULA

The moment of inertia of the flywheel about its own axis of rotation is given by

$$I = \frac{2mgh - mr^2\omega^2}{\omega^2(1+n/N)}$$

where m is the mass attached to the axle of flywheel, h is the height through which the mass falls, r is the radius of axle of flywheel, ω is the angular velocity of flywheel, n is the number of revolutions made by the flywheel before detachment of mass, and N is the number of revolutions of flywheel made by the flywheel after the detachment of mass.

PROCEDURE

1. Examine the wheel and see that there is the least possible friction. Oil the bearings, if necessary. Also spin the flywheel by hand for at least five minutes in order to warm the bearings. If this is not done the frictional couple will not remain constant during the experiment.
2. Measure the diameter of the axle with vernier calipers at different points and find the mean. Measure also the circumference of the wheel W with a thread.
3. Take a strong and thin string whole length is less than the height of the axle from the floor. Make a loop at its one end and slip it on the pin on the axle. Tie a suitable mass to the other end of the string. Suspend the mass by means of the string so that the loop is just on the point of slipping from the pin. Make a chalk mark on the wheel behind the pointer in this position. Also note the position of the lower surface of the mass m on a scale fixed behind on the wall.
4. Now rotate the wheel and wrap the string uniformly wound the axle so that the mass m is slightly below the rim of the wheel and the chalk mark is again opposite to the pointer. Again note the position of the lower surface of the mass on the scale. If now the mass is allowed to fall, it will descend through a height h before being detached from the pin. Count the number of turns wound round the axle and let it be n. The wheel will thus make n revolutions before the thread is detached.
5. Hold a stop watch in your hand and allow the mass to descend. As soon as the sound of the weight striking to ground is heard, start the stop watch. Count the number of revolutions N made by the flywheel before coming to rest with reference to the chalk mark and note the time t taken for the purpose.

   It is possible that in addition to the complete rotations made by the flywheel, there may be a friction of the rotation. To estimate the friction measure the distance along the circumference by which the chalk mark has advanced beyond the pointer, by means of a thread. Divide this distance by the circumference of the wheel. Repeat the process for the same height and mass, making the wheel to rotate in the opposite direction. Take the observation twice in each case.
6. Repeat the experiment with three different masses, suitably adjusting the height through which the mass falls so that the number of rotations made by the flywheel can be easily counted.

OBSERVATIONS

Vernier constant of the calipers = … cm.
Diameter of the axle = (i) … cm, (ii) … cm, (iii) … cm.
Mean diameter of the axle = …cm.
Mean radius of the axle, r = …cm.

Table 1: Data for moment of inertia of the flywheel

Sr. No.	*Direction of rotation*	*Mass including the hanger m (gm)*	*Height h (cm)*	*n*	*Number of revolutions made by the flywheel after the detachment of mass N*			*Time taken for N revolutions t (sec)*		
					1	*2*	*Mean*	*1*	*2*	*Mean*
1	Clockwise									
	Anticlockwise									
2	Clockwise									
	Anticlockwise									
3	Clockwise									
	Anticlockwise									

CALCULATIONS

First set: Angular velocity, $\omega = \frac{4\pi N}{t}$ **= ...rad/sec.**

Therefore, moment of inertia of the flywheel, $I = \frac{2mgh - mr^2\omega^2}{\omega^2\left(1+\frac{n}{N}\right)}$ **= ... gm-cm².**

Second set: ω **= ... rad/sec.**

I **= ... gm-cm².**

Third set: ω **= ... rad/sec.**

I **= ... gm-cm².**

Mean moment of inertia, I **= ... gm-cm²**

RESULT

Moment of inertia of flywheel about its axis of rotation = ... gm-cm².

PRECAUTIONS AND SOURCES OF ERROR

1. **There should be least possible friction in the flywheel. See that the flywheel starts of its own accord and no push is imparted to it. The mass tied to the end of the cord should be of such a value that it is able to overcome friction at the bearings and thus automatically start falling.**
2. **The length of the string should be less than the height of the axle of the flywheel from the floor.**
3. **The loop slipped over the pin should be loose enough to be detached easily.**
4. **The string should be thin and should be wound evenly.**
5. **The stop-watch should be started just when the string is detached.**

VIVA-VOCE

Q. 1. What do you mean by moment of inertia?

Ans. The moment of inertia of a body about an axis is the sum of the products of the mass and square of the distance of different particles of the body from the axis of rotation.

Q. 2. On what factors does the moment of inertia depend?

Ans. The moment of inertia of a body depends upon the mass of the body as well as the manner in which mass is distributed about the axis of rotation.

Q. 3. What do you mean by radius of gyration?

Ans. The radius of gyration is the square root of the mean square distance of the various particles contained in the body from the axis of rotation.

Q. 4. On what factors does the radius of gyration depend?

Ans. The radius of gyration changes with change of location of the axis of rotation.

Q. 5. What is the S.I. unit of moment of inertia?

Ans. The S.I. unit of moment of inertia is kg-m^2.

Q. 6. What is the physical significance of moment of inertia?

Ans. More is the moment of inertia of a body, the larger is the couple required to produce a given acceleration.

Q. 7. Define moment of inertia in terms of angular momentum.

Ans. The moment of inertia of a body about an axis is numerically equal to angular momentum of the rigid body, when rotating with unit angular velocity about that axis.

Q. 8. Define moment of inertia in terms of kinetic energy of rotation.

Ans. The moment of inertia of a body about an axis of rotation is numerically equal to twice the kinetic energy of rotation of the body, when rotating with unit angular velocity about that axis.

Q. 9. Is there any difference between moment of inertia and rotational inertia?

Ans. No, the moment of inertia is also called rotational inertia.

Q. 10. What is a flywheel and what is its practical advantage?

Ans. A flywheel is a large and heavy wheel through the centre of which passes a long cylindrical axis. The apparatus is such that its centre of gravity lies on its axis of rotation and when it is mounted over ball-bearings, it can be brought to rest at any desired position.

Q. 11. Why should the length of the string be less than the height of the axle from the ground?

Ans. The length of string is so chosen that it gets detached from the axle as soon as bottom of mass is about to reach ground.

Q. 12. About what axis do you find moment of inertia of the flywheel?

Ans. We found out moment of inertia of the flywheel about its own axis of rotation passing through its centre of mass.

Q. 13. In a flywheel, most of the mass is concentrated at the rim. Why?

Ans. Due to this particular shape, the flywheel possesses a large value of moment of inertia for the given mass and the radius. If such a wheel gains or losses some rotational energy, it brings about only a very small change in its angular speed. In this way, a flywheel helps to maintain uniform motion.

Q. 14. What is the method of reducing friction at the ball bearings?

Ans. The lubrication reduces the friction at the ball bearings.

Q. 15. What is the principle of measuring the moment of inertia of a flywheel?

Ans. When a mass attached to a coil wound on the axle of flywheel is allowed to fall there is a loss in its potential energy which in turn is converted into the kinetic energy of falling mass and the kinetic energy of the flywheel etc. Thus we can find the rotational kinetic energy of flywheel. Measuring the angular velocity, we can determine the moment of inertia of a flywheel.

Q. 16. What should be the magnitude of mass to be attached to the cord?

Ans. The mass attached to the cord should be such as is capable to overcome the friction at the ball bearings and thus automatically starts falling. However, the mass should not be too large because then the wheel will rotate very fast and it may not be possible to count the number of rotations made by the flywheel.

Q. 17. Would you prefer a thin or thick cord? Why?

Ans. We shall prefer a thin cord whose thickness is small as compared to the diameter of the axle. If the coil is thick then we shall have to add its thickness to the diameter of axle.

Q. 18. Can you use a metallic wire instead of cord? Why?

Ans. No we cannot use a metallic wire because metals are piable and some work will have to be done in straightening the metal wire when it unwinds itself. As we have not taken into account this work while deriving the formula, we cannot use a metal wire.

❑❑❑

EXPERIMENT 13

AIM

To determine the density of the material of a given wire with the help of a sonometer.

APPARATUS

Sonometer, tuning fork, rubber pad, slotted weights, and screw gauge.

THEORY

A sonometer essentially consists of a metal wire stretched over the bridges *A* and *B* placed on a hollow wooden sound box, about one meter long as shown in Fig. 13.1. One end of the wire is fixed to a peg while the other passes over a frictionless pulley carrying a weight hanger at the other end. The bridges *A* and *B* can slide along the wire to have a suitable desired length of the wire between *AB*. It is important that the base on which string and bridges are mounted should be strong. When the wire is plucked, it sets into vibrations having nodes at the two bridges and antinodes in the middle.

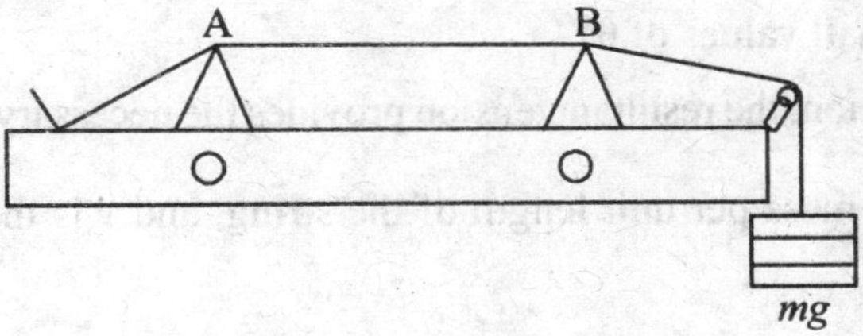

Fig. 13.1 Experimental arrangement

When a stretched string is plucked aside, a wave will travel along its length with a definite velocity. The transverse wave will be propagated to both ends and will be reflected at these points. The incident and reflected waves, traveling to and fro along the string in opposite direction with equal velocities combine to form transverse stationary waves with fixed positions of nodes and anti-nodes.

Consider one portion *APQB* of a string through which a transverse wave is progressing from left to right, as shown in Fig. 13.2. In this case the particles vibrate perpendicular to its length and the movement is handed from one particle to another particle. The velocity of transverse wave will depend on certain constants of the string.

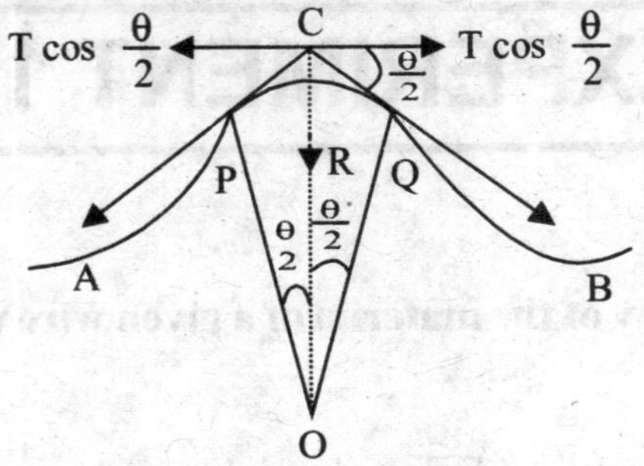

Fig. 13.2 Small portion of string

Consider a small element PQ of the string of length δx and let its centre of curvature be at O. Let $\angle POQ = \theta$. Also consider that the curvature PQ is very small so angle θ is also very small. Let T be tensions at P and Q, the direction of the tensions being tangential to the element P and Q.

Resolve the tensions into horizontal and vertical components. The horizontal components at O are equal and opposite while the perpendicular components are along CO.

Therefore, the resultant tension along CO will be $= \dfrac{2T\sin\theta}{2}$

$$= \frac{2T\theta}{2} = T\theta \text{ (for small values of } \theta) \qquad \text{...(13.1)}$$

For equilibrium position, the resultant tension provides the necessary centripetal force given by $\dfrac{(m\delta x)v^2}{R}$, where m is the mass per unit length of the string, and v is the corresponding velocity.

Therefore,

$$\frac{(m\delta x)v^2}{R} = T\theta$$

Also, $$\theta = \frac{\delta x}{R}$$

On simplification, v is obtained as, $v = \sqrt{\dfrac{T}{m}}$ ...(13.2)

If the string of length l vibrates in p segments, length of each segment being l/p and each segment will correspond to $\lambda/2$. Therefore,

$$\frac{1}{p} = \frac{\lambda}{2} \text{ or } \lambda = \frac{2l}{p}$$

Substituting in the relation $v = n\lambda$, we obtain $v = \dfrac{n(2l)}{p}$ ...(13.3)

Comparing (13.2) and (13.3), we obtain

$$\frac{n(2l)}{p} = \sqrt{\frac{T}{m}}$$

or $$n = \frac{p}{2l}\sqrt{\frac{T}{m}}$$ ...(13.4)

In case the string is vibrating in one segment, then $p = 1$.

Therefore, $$n = \frac{1}{2l}\sqrt{\frac{T}{m}}$$ ...(13.5)

WORKING FORMULA

The frequency n of a tuning fork is given by

$$n = \frac{1}{2l}\sqrt{\frac{T}{m}}$$

where l is the length of the vibrating segment of the sonometer wire, $T = Mg$ is the tension applied to the wire, m is the mass per unit length of the wire, d is the density of the wire, and r is the radius of the wire.

The density of the wire is given by $d = \frac{m}{\pi r^2}$.

PROCEDURE

1. Stretch the wire with a known weight say 1 kg. Arrange the bridges A and B say at a distance of 10 cms from each other. The given tuning fork is now stuck against a pad and hold it above the sonometer wire nearly at midpoint between A and B, so as to excite the wire in the fundamental mode of vibration.
2. Now shift the position of the movable bridges such that a paper rider placed in the middle of the bridges jumps off the wire i.e., in this position the paper rider suited at the antinode and the frequency of the tuning fork is the same as the natural frequency of the wire. Note down the length AB between the bridges at this position.

   This method of ascertaining resonance is not correct one hence the beat method is used. In this method the vibrating tuning fork is moved along the wire slowly till a loud sound is heard showing thereby that we are near the resonance point. Movable bridge is now moved to this point. Again struck the fork and pluck the wire in the middle. Again the notes produced will be slightly different, bets are produced but again the movable arm not adjusted that no beat is heard. The length between the two bridges is noted.
3. Repeat the experiment for different weights.
4. Measure the diameter of sonometer wire with screw gauge from three different positions and take the mean.

OBSERVATIONS

Radius of wire, $r = \ldots$ cm.

Density of the material of wire, $d = \ldots$ gm/cm^3.

Table 1: Determination of *l*

Sr. No	Load (gm)	Length of the wire (cm)
1		
2		
3		
4		

Table 2: Measurement of radius of sonometer wire

Least count of screw gauge = … cm

Zero error of screw gauge = …cm

Sr. No.	Screw gauge readings			Mean diameter (cm)	Radius r = diameter/2 (cm)	Mass per unit length, $m = \pi r^2 d$ (gm/cm)
	M.S.R. (cm)	C.S.R. (cm)	Total (cm)			
1						
2						
3						

CALCULATIONS

Mass per unit length, $m = \pi r^2 d =$ … gm/cm.

First set: Density of given wire, $d = \dfrac{m}{\pi r^2} =$ … gm/cm³.

Second set: Density of given wire, $d = \dfrac{m}{\pi r^2} =$ … gm/cm³.

Third set: Density of given wire, $d = \dfrac{m}{\pi r^2} =$ … gm/cm³.

Mean value of density of sonometer wire = … gm/cm³.

RESULT

The density of sonometer wire determined experimentally = …gm/cm³.

Actual density = … gm/cm³.

Therefore, percentage error = … %.

PRECAUTIONS AND SOURCES OF ERROR

1. The pulley should be frictionless.
2. Wire should be uniform throughout.
3. Weight of the hanger should be included in *T*.
4. After completing the experiment, weights should be removed from the hanger.

VIVA-VOCE

Q. 1. What is a sonometer? Name any instrument working on the same principle used in everyday life.

Ans. A tuning fork is a good laboratory instrument which gives a pure note or a standard frequency. Tuning of radio is based on the principle of resonance.

Q. 2. What is the principle of sonometer?

Ans. It is based on the principle of resonance.

Q. 3. What is resonance?

Ans. When the frequency of the driving force becomes equal to the natural frequency of the oscillator itself, the amplitude of the oscillations becomes very large. Such oscillations are called and this physical phenomenon is called resonance.

Q. 4. Why does the sound become loud when the stem of the tuning fork is pressed on the board?

Ans. The particles of air inside the sonometer vibrate when the stem of the tuning fork is pressed on the board. At resonance their amplitude becomes maximum are sound becomes loud.

Q. 5. What are nodes and antinodes? How do you locate their positions?

Ans. When standing waves are set up in the string, the points where the amplitude are called nodes and the points where amplitude is maximum are called antinodes.

Q. 6. How will the frequency change if the vibrating length of the sonometer wire is doubled and tension is made four times?

Ans. It will remain unchanged.

Q. 7. What are overtones?

Ans. The overtones are notes of higher frequency and are multiples of fundamental note.

Q. 8. If the frequency of the string differs slightly from the frequency of the tuning fork, what will happen?

Ans. Oscillations in the string will die out due to departure from the resonance.

Q. 9. Why does the rider falls down when the frequency of vibration of the wire is equal to that of the tuning fork?

Ans. When the frequency of vibration of the wire is equal to the tuning fork, i.e. at resonance, the wire vibrates with maximum amplitude and hence the rider falls down.

Q. 10. Can you test the position of resonance without using a rider?

Ans. Yes, but not exactly.

Q. 11. What types of vibrations are set up in the sonometer wire and the surrounding air?

Ans. In the sonometer wire transverse stationary waves are set up while in air longitudinal progressive waves are produced.

Q. 12. Why should the pulley be frictionless?

Ans. If friction is present the effective value of tension on the sonometer wire is less than the applied tension, hence the determined density will be different from the actual density.

Q. 13. Why are the stationary waves called so?

Ans. In a stationary wave, the particles of medium vibrate about their mean positions, but disturbance does not travel in any direction.

❑❑❑

EXPERIMENT 14

AIM

To determine the wavelength of prominent spectral lines of mercury by plane diffraction grating in first and second order spectrum.

APPARATUS

Spectrometer, mercury lamp, plane diffraction granting, reading lens, spirit level etc.

THEORY

A plane diffraction grating consists of an optically plane glass plate on which are ruled a number of equidistant, parallel straight lines. The lines divide the glass plate into opacities and transparencies, the thickness of which is of the order of the wavelength of visible light. The region where a line is drawn becomes opaque whereas the space between the two lines is transparent. The number of lines in a plane transmission grating is of the order of 15,000 lines per inch. Fig. 14.1 represents the section of plane transmission grating supposed perpendicular to the plane of the paper. Let the width of the transparency be equal to $AB = a$ and that of the opacity be $BC = b$. The distance $(a+b)$ is called grating element. When a parallel beam of monochromatic light is incident normally on the grating it suffers diffraction. The rays diffracted at an angle θ_n are collected at point P on the screen. The path difference between the rays from two corresponding points A and C is $CN = (a+b)\sin\theta_n$. The same is true for any two corresponding points. The point P will be bright or dark according as the rays reinforce with each other. They would reinforce and give brightness or a maxima if

$$(a+b)\sin\theta_n = n\lambda$$

They will reinforce and give darkness or a minima if

$$(a+b)\sin\theta_n = (2n+1)\frac{\lambda}{2}.$$

When $n = 0$, $\theta_n = 0$. This gives the central bright maximum.

When $n=1$, $(a+b)\sin\theta_1 = \lambda$ and we get the first bright maximum or first order spectrum.

$\therefore$ For first order spectrum, $n=1$ and $(a+b)\sin\theta_1 = \lambda$

Similarly, for second order spectrum, $n=2$ and $(a+b)\sin\theta_2 = 2\lambda$, and so on.

If the light is not monochromatic, then each wavelength gives rise to its won primary maxima in each order. Hence each will consists of a spectrum. The number of lines n per inch are marked on the grating. The value of gratting element is given by

$$(a+b) = \frac{2.54}{N}\text{ cm.}$$

When the number of lines per cm is given, $(a+b) = \frac{1}{N}$ cm.

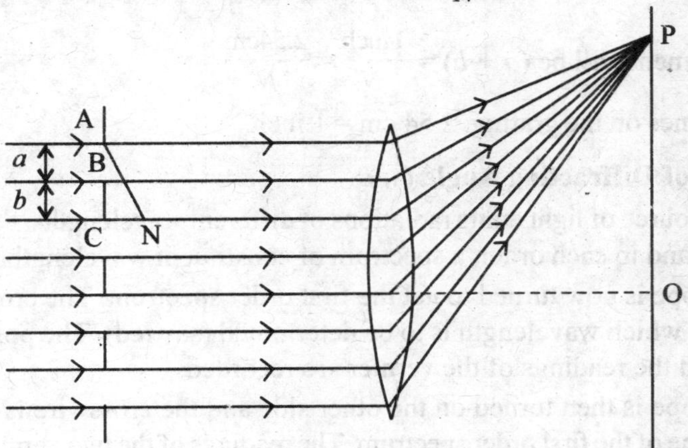

Fig. 14.1 Plane diffraction grating

WORKING FORMULA

The wavelength of a spectral line is given by

$$\lambda = \frac{(a+b)\sin\theta}{n}$$

where $(a + b)$ is granting element (cm), θ is angle of diffraction, n is order of the spectrum

PROCEDURE

Before performing the experiment, the following adjustments are made.

1. Setting the Grating for Normal Incidence

(a) The spectrometer is well adjusted for parallel beam using the usual procedure of seeing a far object.

(b) The position of the telescope is adjusted in such a way that the image of the slit is focussed on the vertical crosswire of the telescope. In this position, the collimator and the telescope are in the same line. The reading is noted on the circular scale.

(c) The telescope is now turned through 90° and clamped.

(d) Grating is now mounted on the prism table normal to the collimator. The prism table is now rotated, so that the image of the slit reflected from the grating surface lies at the intersection of the crosswire.

(e) Prism table is now rotated through an angle of 45° or 135° as the case may be, so that it becomes normal to the incident light. The slit of the collimator is also adjusted, so that sharp spectral lines parallel to the rulings of the grating are formed. The prism table is clamped in this position.

2. Determination of Diffracting Element (a + b)

On every grating, number of rulings (lines) per inch are marked by the manufacturer.

Thus grating element will be $(a+b) = \frac{1\,\text{inch}}{N} = \frac{2.54\text{cm}}{N}$

N = number of lines on the grating, 2.54 cm = 1 inch.

3. Determination of Diffracting Angle (θ)

(a) When the source of light emits radiations of different wavelengths, the beam gets dispersed by grating and in each order, a spectrum of constituent wavelengths is observed.

(b) The telescope is now turned to get the first order spectrum. The cross wire is adjusted on the line for which wavelength is to be determined (say red). The position of the telescope is fixed and the readings of the vernier are recorded.

(c) The telescope is then turned on the other side and the crosswire is adjusted on the same coloured line of the first order spectrum. The readings of the two verniers are again recorded.

(d) The differences of the readings of the same vernier gives twice the angle of diffraction for that lines in the first order. The average of two vernier is taken.

(e) Procedure (b) to (d) is repeated for other lines and for other orders. The arrangement is shown in figure 14.2. Thus knowing grating element $(a + b)$, diffraction angle θ_n and order of spectrum n, one can compute the wavelength of desired spectral line.

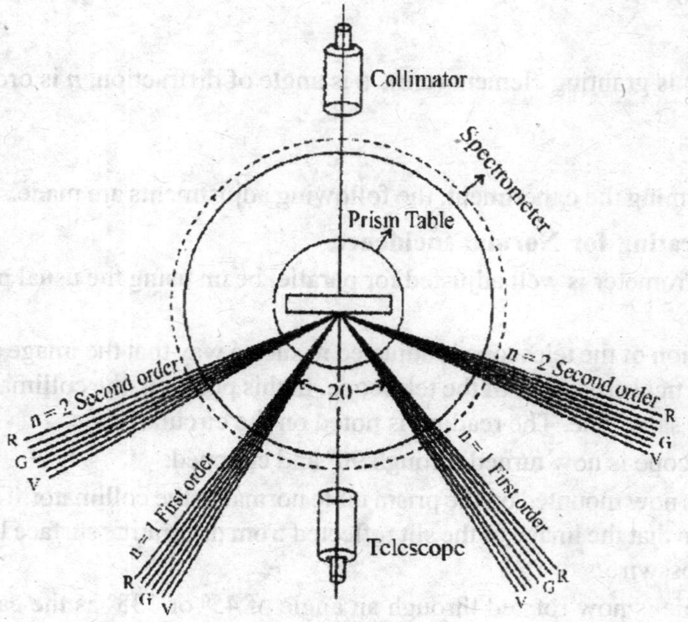

Fig. 14.2 Determination of wavelength of light by plane transmission grating

Observations

(i) Grating element:

Number of lines on grating = 15,000 per inch

Grating element $(a + b) = \frac{2.54}{15,000} = 1.69\times10^{-4}\,cm$

(ii) Angle of diffraction θ :

Least count of main scale x = ...cm.

Number of divisions on the vernier scale m = ...

Least count of vernier scale $= \frac{x}{m} =$ ...... cm.

Table 1: Measurement of angle of diffraction (θ)

Order of the spectrum	*Colour of the spectral line*	*Vernier*	*Spectrum to the left of the direct image*			*Spectrum to the right of the direct image*			$2\theta = \theta_1 - \theta_2$	*Mean* θ
			MSR	*VSR*	*Total* (θ_1)	*MSR*	*VSR*	*Total* (θ_2)		
First Order (n = 1)	Violet	V_1								
		V_2								
	Yellow	V_1								
		V_2								
	Green	V_1								
		V_2								
Second order (n = 2)	Violet	V_1								
		V_2								
	Yellow	V_1								
		V_2								
	Green	V_1								
		V_2								

CALCULATIONS

1. For first order n = 1

(a) Wavelength of violet colour, $\lambda_v = \frac{(a+b)\sin\theta_v}{1} =$ ....Å

(b) Wavelength of yellow colour, $\lambda_y = \frac{(a+b)\sin\theta_y}{1} =$ ....Å

(c) Wavelength of green colour, $\lambda_g = \frac{(a+b)\sin\theta_g}{1} =$ ....Å

2. For second order $n = 2$

(a) Wavelength of violet colour, $\lambda_v = \dfrac{(a+b)\sin\theta_v}{2} = ...\text{Å}$

(b) Wavelength of yellow colour, $\lambda_y = \dfrac{(a+b)\sin\theta_y}{2} = ...\text{Å}$

(c) Wavelength of green colour, $\lambda_g = \dfrac{(a+b)\sin\theta_g}{2} = ...\text{Å}$.

RESULT

For mercury light the mean wavelength of different colours are:

S. No.	Observed	Standard	Percentage Error
1.	λ_v = ...Å	λ_v = 4078 Å	
2.	λ_y = ...Å	λ_y = 5770 Å	
3.	λ_g = ...Å	λ_g = 4960 Å	

PRECAUTIONS AND SOURCES OF ERROR

1. Grating should be set normal to the incident light
2. The slit should be as narrow as possible.
3. Grating should not be touched by fingers.
4. The reading lens should be used for taking readings.
5. The reading of both verniers should be taken.
6. The height of the prism table should be so adjusted that the light must fall on the entire ruling surface of the grating.

VIVA–VOCE

Q.1 What is diffraction?

Ans. The phenomenon of bending of waves around the obstacle and entering in the region of the geometrical shadow of the obstacle is called diffraction of waves.

Q.2 What is diffraction grating?

Ans. Diffraction grating is a plane glass plate on which a large number of equidistant, parallel and fine lines are drawn by means of a fine diamond point worked with a ruling engine.

Q.3 How many types of grating are there?

Ans. There are two types of gratings: (i) transmission grating and (ii) reflection grating.

Q.4 What is grating element?

Ans. The distance between the midpoints of two successive slits is called granting element. This is denoted by $(a + b)$ in the granting formula where a is the width of transport part and b is opaque separation between slits.

Q.5 What is the effect of increasing the number of lines per cm on the grating?

Ans. If the number of lines per cm on the grating is increased, the angle of diffraction θ, for a particular order of the spectrum, increases. This results in a less number of spectra separated by a large angle.

Q.6 How many lines are drawn on a grating?

Ans. The numbers of lines drawn on a grating varies from 10,000 to 15,000 per inch and the width of ruled surface from 2 to 4 inches.

Q.7 What will happen if the rulings of the grating are not parallel and the distance between two successive rulings is not constant?

Ans. Then additional lines will appear near the actual spectral lines which are called 'ghost lines'.

Q.8 Why do you keep the ruled surface towards the telescope?

Ans. If the ruled surface is towards the telescope, the light falling normally on the glass plate enters it undeviated and then only diffraction takes place at the ruled surface. In this case the angle measured will be true angle of diffraction.

Q.9 How many orders can be obtained with the help of grating?

Ans. $n_{max} = \frac{(a+b)}{\lambda}$ depending upon the grating element and the wavelength of light.

Q.10 Are the intensities of light equal in all orders of the spectrum?

Ans. No, the intensity fo spectrum decreases as the orders of spectrum increases.

Q.11 Why do you adjust the grating normal to the incident light ?

Ans. Grating formula $(a+b)\sin\theta = n\lambda$ has been deduced on the condition that the incident wave falls normally on the grating.

Q.12 What are the requisites of a good grating ?

Ans. The lines should be exactly equal, parallel and should be equispaced over the entire ruled space.

Q.13 What will happen to the angular dispersion if the number of lines in the same space be doubled ?

Ans. Since the angular dispersion in inversely proportional to the grating element. Therefore, the angular dispersion will increase as the number of lines increase in the same space.

Q.14 What will happen when the width of lines on grating become equal to the spacing between them ?

Ans. The spectra of even order (n = 2, 4, 6, 8......) will be absent.

Q.15 What is the difference between the spectra formed by a prism and a grating ?

Ans. The order of colours in the two cases is opposite.

Q.16 Why is the intensity of prism spectrum more than that of grating spectrum?

Ans. In case of prism the whole dispersed light is concentrated in one spectrum where as in case of grating the whole light is distributed over the different orders of the spectrum. However, the resolution is better in case of spectrum by grating.

□□□

EXPERIMENT 15

AIM

To determine the thickness of the given wire using wedge method.

APPARATUS

Two optically flat glass plates of same size, sodium lamp, traveling microscope, wooden frame and one glass plate inclined at 45°, a thin wire whose thickness is to be determined.

THEORY

When a thin wire is placed between the two glass plates such that the plates touch at one end and are separated at the other end, a wedge shaped film is formed between them. When a monochromatic light is incident on such a system normally, interference takes place at the wedge shaped air film and fringes are observed with a traveling microscope. The experimental arrangement is shown in Fig. 15.1. A highly magnified view is shown in Fig. 15.2.

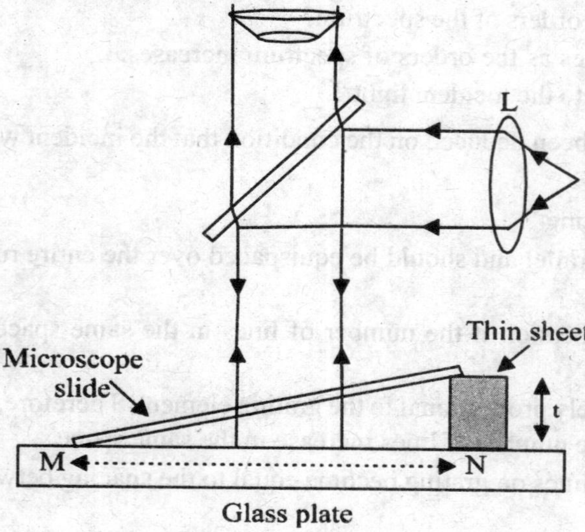

Fig. 15.1 Experimental arrangement

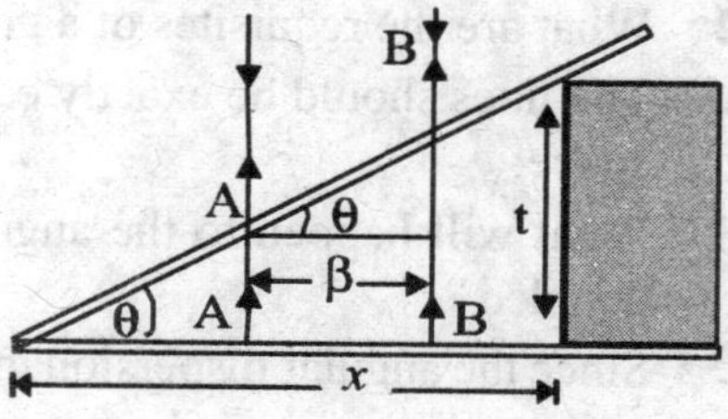

Fig. 15.2 Magnified view

The fringes at *A* is produced by the light beam reflected at *A*, the point at the bottom of the microscope slip and at the pint *A'* immediately below *A* across the air film. The next fringe is produced when the air film has increased in thickness by $\lambda/2$. If θ is the angle of the air wedge, then

$$\tan\theta = \frac{BC}{AC} = \frac{BC}{A'B'} = \frac{\lambda}{2} \times \frac{1}{\beta} \qquad ...(15.1)$$

where β is the fringe width. If t is the thickness of the wire, then

$$\tan\theta = \frac{d}{x} \quad ...(15.2)$$

Therefore

$$\frac{d}{x} = \frac{\lambda}{2\beta}$$

or

$$d = \frac{\lambda x}{2\beta}. \quad ...(15.3)$$

WORKING FORMULA

The diameter (thickness) of the wire is given by

$$d = \frac{\lambda x}{2\beta}$$

where λ is the wavelength of light used, x is the distance between point of contact of two glass plates and the axis of wire fixed between them, and β is the fringe width.

PROCEDURE

1. Level the microscope table, and adjust the microscope tube in a vertical position and find the vernier constant of the horizontal scale.
2. Arrange the apparatus as shown in Fig. 15.1. Place the given wire between the two glass plates such that the glass plates touch at one end and are separated at the other end. Adjust the source and the microscope until parallel interference fringes are formed in the air wedge and seen in the field of view of the microscope and the vertical cross-wire coincides with the centre of the straight fringes. Note the reading of the microscope vernier on the scale in this position.
3. Slide the microscope to one side with the help of slow motion screw and set it on the next 5th fringe. Note the reading again.
4. Repeat the experiment for 10th, 15th, ...30th fringes and find the fringe width *â*.
5. Now measure the distance x of the edge of thin plate from the line of contact of the microscope slide with the glass plate at M and N with the help of traveling microscope. Repeat three times.

OBSERVATIONS

Vernier constant = ... cm.

Wavelength of sodium light = 5893×10^{-8} cm.

Table 1: Determination of fringe width *β*

Sr. No.	No. of fringes	Microscope reading M.S.R. (cm)	Microscope reading V.S.R. (cm)	Microscope reading Total (cm)	Width of 5 fringes (cm)	Mean of 5 fringes x (cm)	Fringe width $\beta = x/15$ (cm)
1	0				>		
2	5				>		
3	10				>		
4	15				>		
5	20				>		
6	25				>		
7	30						

Mean β = … cm.

Table 2: Measurement of Mean value

Sr. No.	Microscope reading on Thin plate N: M.S.R. (cm)	V.S.R. (cm)	Total a (cm)	Microscope reading on Line of contact M: M.S.R. (cm)	V.S.R. (cm)	Total b(cm)	$x = b - a$ (cm)
1							
2							
3							

Mean value of x = … cm

CALCULATIONS

The thickness of the given wire, $d = \dfrac{\lambda x}{2\beta}$ = … cm.

RESULT

The thickness of the given wire = … cm

PRECAUTIONS AND SOURCES OF ERROR

1. The wire used should be thin and should be fixed at one end of the glass plate.
2. The glass plates should be very clean and optically flat.
3. The source of light used should be an extended one.
4. Crosswire should be focused on a dark fringe.
5. The microscope should be moved in the same direction while taking the observations for fringes.

VIVA-VOCE

Q. 1. On which phenomenon of light waves, this experiment is based?

Ans. Interference of light

Q. 2. What do you mean by interference of light?

Ans. The redistribution of light energy obtained by the superposition of light waves from the sources of light is called interference of light.

Q. 3. What are coherent sources?

Ans. Two sources of light are said to be coherent if they emit light waves continuously of same frequency and the two waves either in same phase or have a constant phase difference.

Q. 4. How coherent sources are obtained in this experiment?

Ans. The waves reflected from the upper and lower surfaces of the thin air film formed between the two glass plates acts as two coherent sources.

Q. 5. What is wedge shaped film?

Ans. A film of variable thickness is known as wedge shaped film.

Q. 6. What is the condition of maxima and minima in interference pattern?

Ans. For maxima the effective path difference between the interfering waves is integral multiple of wavelength of light and for minima the effective path difference between the interfering waves is odd integral multiple of half of wavelength of light.

Q. 7. What is Stoke's treatment?

Ans. When a ray of light reflected at the surface of a denser medium, it suffers a phase change of π or path difference of $\lambda/2$ is introduced in it.

Q. 8. What is the effective path difference between the interfering rays in this experiment?

Ans. The effective path difference between the interfering rays in this experiment (reflected system) is $2\mu t \cos\{r+\alpha\}-\lambda/2$, where μ is the refractive index of air film, t is thickness of air film, r is angle of refraction, α is angle of wedge, and λ is the wavelength of light.

Q. 9. What type of fringes is obtained in this experiment?

Ans. Fringes of equal thickness are obtained. Such fringes are called localized fringes.

Q. 10. What are localized fringes?

Ans. Fringes of equal thickness are called localized fringes.

Q. 11. Why extended source is required to observe the fringes?

Ans. With a point source of light only a small portion of film will be visible. In case of extended source of light a large portion of the film is accommodated by the eye and the field of view is large. Due to this reason we always need an extended source of light to observe interference in thin films.

Q. 12. Why the glass plate is inclined at 45° with the vertical?

Ans. With this arrangement, the light incidents on the wedge shaped film normally, hence angle of refraction $r = 0°$.

❑❑❑

EXPERIMENT 16

AIM

To determine the wavelength of He-Ne laser light using single slit.

APPARATUS

He-Ne gas laser source, grating, optical bench, screen.

THEORY

Laser: The name Laser is an acronym of "Light Amplification by Stimulated. Emission of Radiation." A laser is a device that produces an intense, concentrated and highly parallel beam of coherent light.

The transition of energy (atom) in a system can occur in two ways. In one way, the atom can absorb energy and go to higher energy level (or become excited). In another way, it can also come back to the lower energy level by liberating energy (emission or dexcitation). Thus the transfer of energy can take place by either absorption or emission. Emission or dexcitation of atom can occur by spontaneous or stimulated emission.

The rate of transition of atoms by absorption of radiation is equal to the rate of transition by emission of radiation. In the presence of incident radiations (photons) the equilibrium is disturbed and the ratio of emission and absorption rates is given by following equation:

$$\frac{\text{Emission rate}}{\text{Absorption rate}} = \frac{R_{21}}{R_{12}} = \frac{\left[A_{21} + B_{21}u(v)\right]N_2}{B_{12}u(v)N_1} \quad \text{...(16.1)}$$

Since $B_{12} = B_{21}$

$$\text{Therefore } \frac{R_{21}}{R_{12}} = \left[1 + \frac{A_{21}}{B_{21}u(v)}\right] \times \frac{N_2}{N_1} \quad \text{...(16.2)}$$

For laser action, two conditions should be satisfied

(i) The probability of spontaneous emission which produces incoherent radiations should be much smaller than the probability of stimulated radiation i.e. $A_{21} << B_{21}u(v)$ or stimulated emission.

Thus, with this condition equation (16.2) becomes

$$\frac{\text{Emission rate}}{\text{Absorption rate}} = \frac{N_2}{N_1} \quad \text{...(16.3)}$$

(ii) The emission rate should be larger than the absorption rate.

Helium-neon Laser: An early from of He-Ne laser is shown in figure 16.1. The He-Ne laser uses' a mixture of Helium and Neon in the ratio of 10:1, kept in a narrow pyrex glass tube with an internal diameter of 2 mm and length of about 40 cm.

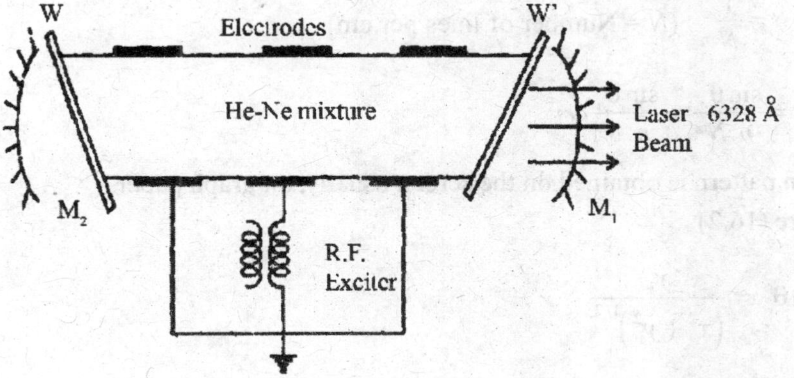

Fig. 16.1 He-Ne gas laser

The helium gas is filled at a pressure of 1 torr and neon at a pressure of about 0.1 torr. The gas system is enclosed between the pair of mirrors. The window WW' cemented at Brewster angle at the end of discharge tube, are of borosilicate glass and optically flat (to about one tenth of wavelength). The reflectors M_1M_2 are two dielectric coated spherical mirrors having a high reflectivity at 6328 $\mathring{A}$. One mirror acts a perfect reflector and the other is partly transparent for the emergence of laser light. Thus, a cavity resonator system is formed. The spacing between the mirrors is equal to an integral number of half wavelength of laser light. Pumping is achieved by an electrical discharge produced in the gas by means of electrodes placed outside the tube connected to a source of high frequency alternating current.

Determine the wavelength of laser light: Monochromatic radiations of wavelength ë is diffracted by a diffraction grating. The formation of maxima take place on the screen. The nth order principal maxima (figure 16.2) formed at an angle θ_n given by

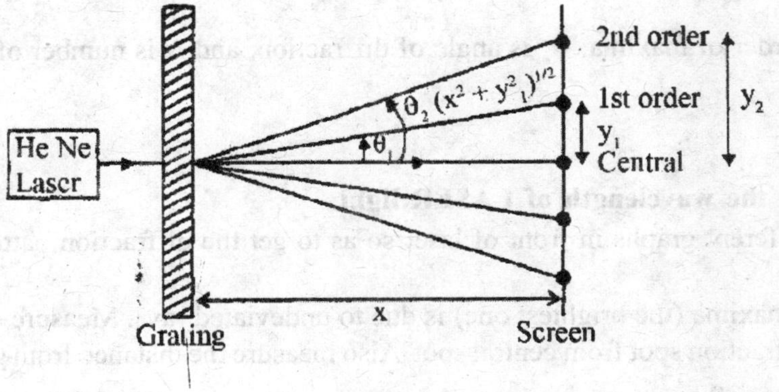

Fig. 16.2

$$(a+b)\sin\theta_n = n\lambda$$

where $(a+b)$ is the grating element given by ...(16.4)

$$a+b = \frac{1}{N} \quad (N = \text{Number of lines per cm})$$

$$\therefore \quad \lambda = \frac{\sin\theta_n}{n.N} = \frac{\sin\theta_n}{n.N} cm \qquad ...(16.5)$$

Diffraction pattern is obtained on the screen usually, on graph paper.

From figure (16.2)

$$\sin\theta_n = \frac{y_n}{\left(x^2+y_n^2\right)^{1/2}}$$

so,

$$\lambda = \frac{y_n}{\left(x^2+y_n^2\right)^{1/2}} \cdot \frac{1}{Nn} cm$$

Again from equation (16.5)

$$\sin\theta_n = (N\lambda).n$$

i.e. graph between $\sin\theta_n$ and n should be a straight line having slope = $N\lambda$

Thus, a graph will be plotted between $\sin\theta_n$ and n, and

$$\text{slop of graph} = \frac{\Delta(\sin\theta_n)}{\Delta n}$$

WORKING FORMULA

$$\text{Wavelength of laser beam } \lambda = \frac{(\text{slope of graph between } \sin\theta_n \text{ and } n)}{N}$$

where n is order of maxima, θ_n is angle of diffraction, and N is number of lines per cm on grating.

PROCEDURE

(a) To determine the wavelength of LASER light

1. Place different graphs in front of laser so as to get the diffraction pattern on the graph paper.
2. Central maxima (the brightest one) is due to undeviated rays. Measure distances of first order diffraction spot from central spot. Also measure the distance from grating to screen. Calculate $\sin\theta_1$.

$$\therefore \quad \text{slope of graph} = \frac{\Delta \sin\theta_n}{\Delta n} = \lambda N$$

Hence, wavelength of Laser Beam is $\lambda = \dfrac{(\text{slope of graph})}{N}$ ...(16.6)

3. **Repeat step 2th for second and third order diffraction spot to find $\sin\theta_2$ and $\sin\theta_3$. Hence plot the graph between $\sin\theta_n$ vs n and calculate λ as per as equation 16.6.**

Table 1: Observation table for determination of wavelength

S. No.	*Order of Diffraction n*	*Position of Screen x (cm)*	*Distance of Diffraction Spot from Central Spot y (cm)*	*sin θ* $= y_n/(x^2+y_n^2)^{1/2}$
1	0			
2	1			
3	2			
4	3			

Distance of screen from grating (D) = ... cm.

CALCULATIONS

Gratting constant $(a+b) = \dfrac{1}{N}$

or $N = \dfrac{1}{a+b}$ per cm

Distance of screen from Grating (D) = ...

Slope of graph between $\sin\theta_n$ vs n

$$\frac{\Delta \sin\theta_n}{\Delta n} = ...$$

$$\therefore \quad \lambda = \frac{\Delta(\sin\theta_n)}{\Delta n}\cdot\frac{1}{N} = \text{....cm}$$

$$= \text{.......} \mathring{A}$$

RESULT

The wavelength of He-Ne Laser = ... Å

Standard value of wavelength of He-Ne Laser = 6328 Å

Percentage error = ...

PRECAUTION AND SOURCES OF ERROR

1. Laser source and screen should be at the same height on the optical bench.
2. Hole in front of Laser should be very small.
3. Do not look directly at laser beam because it may damages eyes.
4. Laser source is to be switched off after taking observation.

VIVA-VOCE

Q. 1 What are the characteristic of laser source?

Ans. Laser light is coherent, very intense, highly directional monochromatic light.

Q. 2 What do you understand by active medium?

Ans. The active LASER medium consists of a collection of atoms, molecules or ions. The excited state of the active laser medium must be having at least on a metastable state which means its life must be long compared to the usually short life time of excited states.

Q. 3 What is optical resonator?

Ans. For laser action to occur high photon density is required, this is achieved by the use of reflecting parallel mirror at the end of the system; one of them is totally reflector and another is partially reflector.

Q. 4 What is the wavelength width of laser emission?

Ans. The wavelength width of the LASER, emission is found in the range of 10^{-7} Å to 10^{-2} Å

Q. 5 What is the difference between Ordinary, Mercury and Laser light?

Ans. Ordinary light is not coherent in nature (incoherent light source)

Laser light is coherent, monochromatic highly intense and have directionality. Mercury source produces light emitting in all direction while laser source produces light emitting in only one direction. Light from mercury source when passes through grating produces line spectrum while light from laser source produce spots.

Q. 6 What are the conditions for LASER production?

Ans. For laser action two condition must be satisfied

(i) The emission rate must be larger than the absorption rate.

(ii) The probability for stimulated emission must be larger than the probability for spontaneous emission.

Q. 7 What do you mean by gas laser?

Ans. A laser in which the active medium is a gas containing a laser active species. It is typically composed of a plasma discharge tube containing a gas that can be excited with an electric discharge.

Q. 8 What is population inversion and how it is achieved?

Ans. Population Inversion: Normally the number of atoms at high energy level (E_2) is less than those in low energy level $(E_1), N_2(E_2) < N_1(E_1)$. If $N_2 > N_1$, we say population inversion exists, which is necessary condition for lasing.

Q. 9 What is the meastable state?

Ans. Metastable state is excited state of an atom, nucleus, or other system that has a longer lifetime than the ordinary excited state and generally has a shorted lifetime than the ground state. In quantum mechanical terms, transitions from metastable states are "forbidden" and much less probable than the "allowed" transitions from other excited states.

Q. 10 What is optical pumpitng?

Ans. The process to raise atoms from lower level to upper level is called pumping.

Q. 11 What are the basic types of laser?

Ans. LASER can be divided in to three types based on their lasing

(i) Solid state Laser: Ruby Laser

(ii) Gaseous Laser: He-Ne Laser

(iii) Diode Laser: Ga-As semiconductor Laser and LED.

Q. 12 What are the difference between He-Ne laser and semiconductor laser?

Ans. (i) He-Ne laser requires 10 to 20W of energy to produce a few milli Watts of light, while semiconductor laser typically require less than 0.5W of energy.

(ii) He-Ne lasers limit users to half a dozen or so wavelengths, while laser diodes provide and abundance of available wavelengths in the ultraviolet, visible, and infrared.

Q. 13 What are the practical applications of Laser?

Ans. Practical Applications

1. In Medical: A laser beam guided by the fiber is used to reattach detached retinas and to correct defects in vision. As optical fibre can be bent in any shape and no obstruction is found in the propagation of light through the fiber. In can be used to a variety of medical needs.
2. For delivering light from a source to a remote or in accessible point.
3. Laser beam is used in 3-dimensional image creation and dimensional photography.
4. LASER has an important hole in reading and writing of compact discs.
5. The distance of astronomical bodies like moon, planets and many of the galaxies have been measured precisely by using laser beam.

❑❑❑

EXPERIMENT 17

AIM

To determine the frequency of an electrically maintained tuning fork by Melde's method.

APPARATUS

Electrically maintained tuning fork, a stand with clamp, pulley, a light weight pan, a weight box, a balance, a battery of two cells, a key, a rheostat, connecting wires etc.

THEORY

The apparatus consists of a light string *AB* of uniform diameter and about one meter long, one end of which is connected to the prong of an electrically maintained tuning fork and the other end after passing over a frictionless pulley is connected to a light scale pan *P*. The tension in the string can be varied by placing different weights in the pan. Stationary waves are produced due to the superimposition of the direct waves sent by the tuning fork and the reflected waves from the pulley.

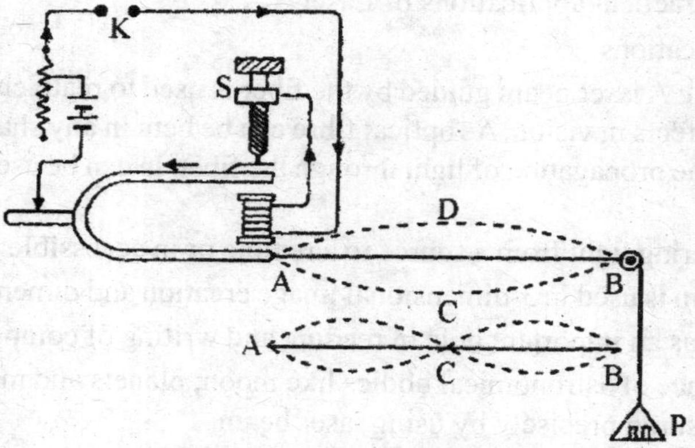

Fig. 17.1 Transverse arrangement

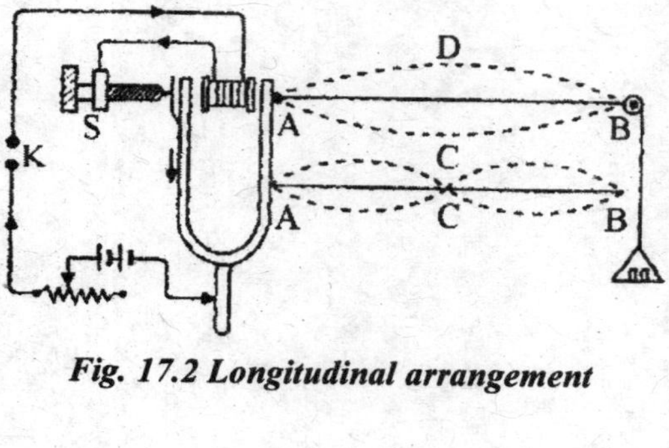

Fig. 17.2 Longitudinal arrangement

There are two modes of vibrations:

(a) Transverse mode of vibration: In this arrangement the vibrations of the prong of the tuning fork are in a direction perpendicular to the length of the string as shown in Fig. 17.1. The time during which the tuning fork completes one vibration, the string also completes one vibration. If the thread of length l vibrates in one loop, the frequency of the fundamental note under a tension T is given by

$$n=\frac{1}{2l}\sqrt{\frac{T}{m}} \quad \text{....(17.1)}$$

where m is the mass per unit length of the thread. If the same length vibrates in N-loops under a tension T_N, then

$$n=\frac{N}{2l}\sqrt{\frac{T_N}{m}} \quad \text{...(17.2)}$$

From (17.1) and (17.2), we obtain

$$\frac{T_N}{T}=\frac{1}{N^2} \text{ or } T_N=\frac{T}{N^2}$$

Thus if we wish to have N-loops in the same length of the string, the tension should be reduced to $1/N^2$ of its previous length.

(b) Longitudinal mode of vibration: In this arrangement the tuning fork is set in such a manner that the vibrations of the prongs are parallel to the length of the string as shown in Fig. 2. In this case the time, during which the tuning fork completes one vibration, the string completes half a vibration. Hence the frequency of the thread is half that of the tuning fork. If the same length l of the thread vibrates in one loop under a tension T, then

Frequency of fork $n = 2\times$frequency of the string

$$=2\times\frac{1}{2l}\sqrt{\frac{T}{m}}=\frac{1}{l}\sqrt{\frac{T}{m}}$$

where m is the mass per unit length of the string. For N-loops the frequency

$$n=\frac{N}{l}\sqrt{\frac{T_N}{m}}$$

Thus if the same length of the thread vibrates under the same tension in the two modes of vibration, the number of loops in the transverse arrangement is double as compared to the number of loops in the longitudinal mode of vibration.

WORKING FORMULA

For the transverse arrangement, the frequency of the tuning fork is given by

$$n=\frac{1}{2l}\sqrt{\frac{T}{m}}=\frac{1}{2l}\sqrt{\frac{Mg}{m}}$$

For the longitudinal arrangement, the frequency of the tuning fork is given by

$$n = \frac{1}{l}\sqrt{\frac{T}{m}} = \frac{1}{l}\sqrt{\frac{Mg}{m}}$$

where l is the length of the thread in the fundamental vibration, T is the tension applied to thread, M is the total mass suspended, and m is the mass per unit length of the thread.

PROCEDURE

Transverse Arrangement

1. Find the weight of the pan and arrange the apparatus as shown in Fig. 17.1.
2. Place a load of 20 gm in the pan attached to the end of the string passing over the pulley. Excite the tuning fork by putting the plug in the key K.
3. Adjust the position of the pulley so that the string is set into resonant vibrations and well defined loops are obtained. If necessary, adjust the tension by adding weights in the pan slowly and gradually. For finer adjustment add milligram weights so that the nodes are reduced to points.
4. Measure the length of loops formed N in the string. If L is the distance in which N loops are formed then distance between two consecutive nodes, $l = L/N$.
5. Note down the weight placed in the pan and calculate the tension T. Tension T = (weights in the pan + weight of pan) g.
6. Repeat the experiment twice by changing the weight in the pan in steps of one gram and altering the position of the pulley each time to get well defined loops.
7. Measure one meter length of the thread and find its mass to find the value of m, the mass per unit length.

Longitudinal Arrangement

Set the apparatus as shown in Fig. 17.2 and proceed with the adjustments and measurements as explained above.

OBSERVATIONS

Mass of pan, w = ... gm = ... kg.

Mass of one meter of thread = ...gm = ... kg.

Mass per meter, m =...... gm = ...kg.

Table 1: Determination of frequency of tuning fork

Mode of vibration	*No.*	*No. of loops (N)*	*Length of corresponding thread L (m)*	*Length of each loop L/N = l (m)*	*Mass in the pan W (kg)*	*Tension =(W + W)g*	*Frequency*
Transverse (A)	1						
	2						
	3						
Longitudinal (B)	1						
	2						
	3						

CALCULATIONS

A. Transverse arrangement: Mean value of frequency of tuning fork = ... Hz.

B. Longitudinal arrangement: Mean value of frequency of tuning fork = ... Hz.

PRECAUTIONS AND SOURCES OF ERROR

1. The thread should be uniform and inextensible.
2. The thread should be horizontal and in alignment with the tuning fork. In transverse arrangement the thread should be stretched in line with the length of the prong so that the vibrations of the tip of the prong are at right angles to it. In the longitudinal arrangement the thread should be in line with the vibration of the prong.
3. Well defined loops should be obtained by adjusting the tension with milligram weights.
4. Friction in the pulley should be least possible as otherwise it causes the tension to be less than the applied tension.
5. The loops in the central part of the thread should be counted for measurements. The nodes at the tip of the prong and at the pulley should be neglected as these have same motion.
6. The friction at the pulley and sparking at the platinum points cannot be totally eliminated.
7. There is a change in frequency due to the clamping screw at the tip of the prong of the tuning fork.

VIVA-VOCE

Q. 1. What is an electrically maintained tuning fork?

Ans. It is a device which produces periodic vibrations due to electrical supply of energy.

Q. 2. What do you mean by an ideal string?

Ans. An ideal string is an infinitely thin, perfectly flexible cord having a uniform diameter throughout.

What ... types of waves are produced in this experiment?

... waves.

Q. 4. What ... waves?

Ans. When two wa... ency and amplitude traveling with same velocity in opposite directions in a strai... se upon each other, the resultant wave so formed is known as a stationary wave.

Q. 5. How are the stationary waves produced in this experiment?

Ans. The stationary waves are formed due to superimposition of incident waves moving towards pulley and reflected waves from pulley which travel back to tuning fork.

Q. 6. What do you mean by nodes and antinodes?

Ans. Those points where the displacement of particles of the medium is zero are called nodes while those points where the displacement of particles of the medium is maximum are called antinodes.

Q. 7. What is the longitudinal mode of propagation?

Ans. In this mode, cord is stretched perpendicular to the length of the prongs if the motion of the prongs is along the length of the cord. The frequency of the cord is half that of the tuning fork.

Q. 8. What is the transverse mode of transfer of energy?

Ans. In transverse arrangement, the cord is stretched along the length of the prongs and the motion of prongs is at right angles to the length of the cord. The frequency of the cord is equal to the frequency of the tuning fork.

Q. 9. Can you get different number of loops in the same length of the string?

Ans. Yes, by varying the tension in the string.

Q. 10. What is the relation between the number of loops in the transverse and longitudinal mode for the same tension and length of the string?

Ans. The number of loops in the transverse mode is twice the number of loops in the longitudinal mode.

Q. 11. What is the reason?

Ans. The vibrational frequency of the string in the longitudinal mode is half the vibration of the string in the transverse mode.

Q. 12. What types of waves are produced in the string in transverse and longitudinal mode?

Ans. Transverse stationary waves and longitudinal stationary waves.

Q. 13. Can a rubber or plastic string be used?

Ans. No, because the vibrations die very quickly in their case as they are not rigid.

Q. 14. Can you verify the laws of vibrations of a stretched string by Melde's experiment?

Ans. Yes, we can verify all the laws of string.

❑❑❑

EXPERIMENT 18

AIM

To study the variation of magnetic field along the axis of Helmholtz coil and to find the reduction factor.

APPARATUS

Helmholtz galvanometer, battery eliminator, rheostat, ammeter, a commutator, plug key and connecting wires.

THEORY

Helmholtz galvanometer consists of two circular coils of equal radius and having equal number of turns of insulated wires fixed with their planes vertical on a horizontal bench graduated in cm. A magnetometer compass box can slide on the bench such that the centre of the needle always lies on the common axis of the coils as shown in Fig. 18.1.

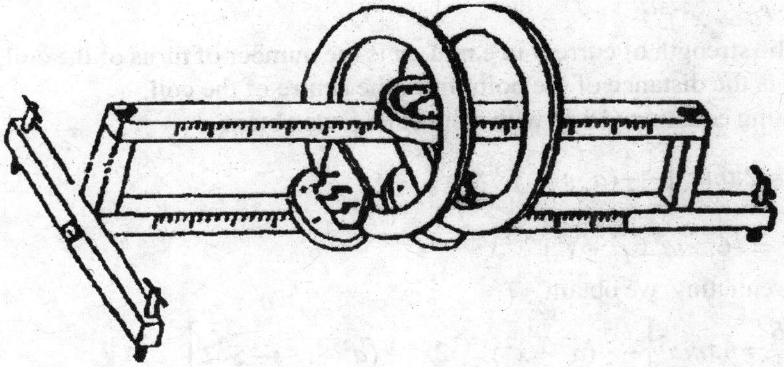

Fig. 18.1 Helmholtz galvanometer

Let the planes of the two coils are perpendicular to the plane of paper and O_1 and O_2 are the centers of these coils. Now, since both the coils have current in the same direction, so the magnetic field at any point on their common axis will be in the same direction due to these two coils.

If a point shifts from O_1 to O_2, the magnetic field due to first coil will decrease and that due to second increases. The distance between the centers of the two coils is adjusted in such a way that the rate of increase of magnetic field due to one coil is equal to rate of decrease due to the other coil. In this way the resultant intensity at any point due to the current passing through the coils will be constant and magnetic field moves in a uniform magnetic field. The variation of magnetic field is shown in Fig. 18.2.

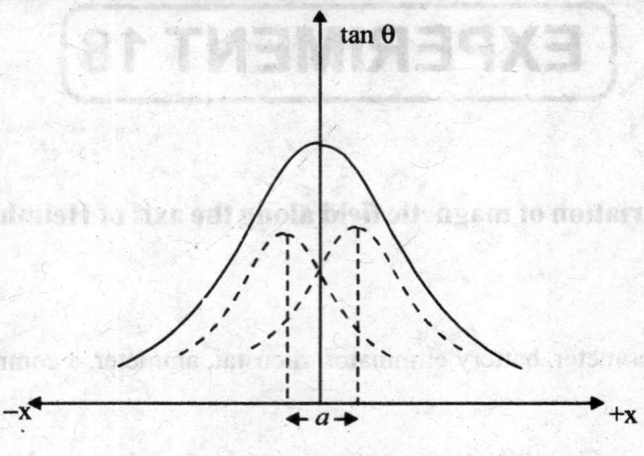

Fig. 18.2 Variation of magnetic field with distance

Now the magnetic field at any point on the axis of a circular coil of wire carrying current is given by

$$B = \frac{2\pi nia^2}{(a^2 + x^2)^{3/2}} \qquad ....(18.1)$$

where i is the strength of current in e.m.u., n is the number of turns of the coil, a is the radius of the coil, and x is the distance of the point from the centre of the coil.

Differentiating equation (18.1) with respect to x, we obtain

$$\frac{dB}{dx} = 2\pi nia^2\left[-\frac{3}{2}(a^2 + x^2)^{-5/2}2x\right]$$

$$= -6\pi nia^2(a^2 + x^2)^{-5/2}x$$

Again differentiating, we obtain

$$\frac{d^2B}{dx^2} = 6\pi nia^2\left[-\frac{5}{2}(a^2 + x^2)^{-7/2}2x^2 + (a^2 + x^2) - 5/2\right]$$

$$= 6\pi nia^2(a^2 + x^2)^{-7/2}(4x^2 - a^2)$$

Since magnetic field along the common axis of coils is uniform, *i.e.* $\frac{dB}{dx}$ is constant or $\frac{d^2B}{dx^2} = 0.$

If $\frac{d^2B}{dx^2} = 0$, then $6\pi nia^2(a^2 + x^2)^{-7/2}(4x^2 - a^2) = 0$

Since $6\pi nia^2 \neq 0$ and $(a^2 + x^2)^{-7/2} \neq 0.$

Therefore $(4x^2 - a^2) = 0$

or $x^2 = \frac{a^2}{4}$ or $x = \pm\frac{a}{2}.$

So in order to get a uniform magnetic field, the magnetic needle should be at a distance $a/2$ from the centre of each of the two coils *i.e.*, the distance between the two coils will be a or $2x$ which means that the distance between the two coils is equal to the radius of either coil.

If the magnetic field due to each coil is B, the resultant magnetic field due to both the coils will be $B_1 = B_2$.

Now in the equilibrium position

$$B_1 = 2B = BH \tan\theta$$

or

$$2\times\frac{2\pi nia^2}{(a^2+x^2)^{3/2}} = B_H \tan\theta$$

Putting $x = \frac{a}{2}$ t

$$\frac{4\pi nia^2}{\left(a^2+\frac{x^2}{4}\right)} = B_H \tan\theta$$

On simplification, we obtain $i = \frac{5\sqrt{5aB_H}\tan\theta}{32\pi n} = k\tan\theta$

where $k = \frac{5\sqrt{5aB_H}}{32\pi n}$, where k is a constant for the galvanometer at a particular place called the reduction factor of the galvanometer.

Therefore, $k = \frac{i}{\tan\theta}$

where k and i are in ampere.

WORKING FORMULA

The reduction factor is given by $k = \frac{i}{\tan\theta}$

where i is the current flowing through the coil and θ is the deflection of the magnetometer needle.

PROCEDURE

1. Place the coils parallel to each other on the sliding bench with a distance a between them, where a is the radius of the coils.
2. Place the magnetometer compass box on the sliding bench so that its magnetic needle is at the midpoint between both the coils. By rotating the whole apparatus in the horizontal plane, set the coils in the magnetic meridian. In this case the coil, the magnet and its image all lie in the same vertical plane. Rotate the compass box till the pointer ends. Read 0-0 on the circular scale.
3. Set up the electrical connections as shown in Fig. 18.2. Send the current in one direction with the help of commutator and note down the deflection. Now reverse the current and again note down

the deflections. If both the deflections are equal then the coils are exactly in magnetic meridian. Otherwise turn the apparatus little, just pointer ends to read 0-0. Repeat the experiment till these deflections become equal.

4. Using rheostat (Rh) adjust the current in ammeter such the deflection of nearly 60° is produced in the compass needle when placed at the midpoint of the coils. Read both the ends of the pointer θ_1 and θ_2. Reverse the direction of the current and again read both the ends of the pointer θ_3 and θ_4. The mean of four readings will give the mean deflection at the centre ($x = 0$).
5. Now shift the compass box through 2 cm along the axis of the coil in one direction and for each position note down the deflection. Continue this process till the deflection becomes very small.
6. Repeat the experiment for the same set of distances on the other side of the coil.
7. Plot a graph to show the variation of magnetic field with distance of circular coil as shown in Fig. 18.2. Taking x along X-axis and tan è along Y-axis.

OBSERVATIONS

Number of turns of the coils, n = ... turns

Least count of the ammeter = ... amp.

Current in ammeter, i = ... amp.

Table 1: Determination of tan θ and distance *x*

S.No.	*Distance of needle from the centre x (cm)*	*Deflection on East arm*							*Deflection on West arm*							
		Current one way		*Current reversed*		*Mean θ*	*θ in degree*	*tan θ*	*Current one way*		*Current reversed*		*Mean θ*	*θ in degree*	*tan θ*
		θ_1	θ_2	θ_3	θ_4				θ_3	θ_4					
1																
2																
3																
4																
5																
6																
7																
8																

CALCULATIONS

At $\theta = 45°$, the reduction factor $k = i$ = ... mA.

RESULT

The graph shows the variation of magnetic field along the axis of a circular coil carrying current.

Reduction factor for the Helmholtz galvanometer = ... mA.

PRECAUTIONS AND SOURCES OF ERROR

1. The connections must be tight.
2. The deflections must lie between 30° and 60°.
3. The coil should be in the magnetic meridian.
4. No magnetic material and current carrying conductors should be brought near the apparatus.
5. The error to parallax in reading the deflection of the needle should always be avoided.
6. Error due to magnetic needle not being pivoted at the centers of the circular scale. The error is eliminated by reading both ends of the pointer.
7. Error due to the galvanometer coil not being exactly in the magnetic meridian. This error is eliminated by recording the deflections for direct as well as for reverse current.

VIVA-VOCE

Q.1. What is the Helmholtz galvanometer?

Ans. A Helmholtz galvanometer consists of two similar coils of wire mounted on the same base and can rotate about a vertical axis. The two coils are connected in series and have got the same radius, the distance between the centers of the two coils being equal to the radius of either coil. A deflection magnetometer box is fitted at the middle point on the line joining the two coils.

Q. 2. What is the principle of Helmholtz galvanometer?

Ans. It is based on the principle of tangent law of magnetism viz; $B = B_H \tan\theta$, where B and B_H are two uniform magnetic fields and θ is the angle between the direction of B_H and direction of magnetic needle when it comes to rest under the influence of the fields B and B_H.

Q. 3. What is magnetic meridian?

Ans. A vertical plane which passes through the imaginary line joining the magnetic north and the south poles is called the magnetic meridian. A magnetic needle, which is free to swing horizontally, would then lie in the magnetic meridian and the north pole of the needle would point towards the magnetic north pole.

Q. 4. Why it is important to set the coil in magnetic meridian.

Ans. The coil is set in the magnetic meridian so that earth's magnetic field does not disturb the magnetic field of the coil.

Q. 5. What is the strength of magnetic field on the axis of the circular coil?

Ans. The strength of magnetic field on the axis of a circular coil is given by $B = \frac{2\pi nia^2}{(a^2 + x^2)^{3/2}}$, where i is the strength of current in e.m.u., n is the number of turns of the coil, a is the radius of the coil, and x is the distance of the point from the centre of the coil.

Q. 6. What is the reduction factor of a galvanometer?

Ans. The reduction factor if a galvanometer is given by $k = i/\tan\theta$.

Q. 7. How the magnetic field will be affected if the number of turns is changed in the circular coil?

Ans. The magnetic field will be increased if the number of turns is increased in the coil.

Q. 8. Why it is necessary to keep the current constant while taking the readings?

Ans. It is necessary to keep the current constant while taking the readings, otherwise the magnetic field will change and hence the deflection.

❑❑❑

EXPERIMENT 19

AIM

To draw the V – I characteristics of a forward and reverse biased PN-Junction diode

APPARATUS

Experimental training board, connecting wires, battery.

THEORY

When a p-type semiconductor is suitably joined to n-type semiconductor, a new crystal is formed which is called diode and contact surface or area is called p-n junction.

Such type of junction can be formed by solid state diffusion or alloying. In solid state diffusion, impurities of one type are diffused into the crystal doped with opposite type of impurity at an appropriate high temperature. In alloying a 'dot' of p-impurity such as Indium is placed on substrate of n-type silicon and this system is heated to high temperature and indium fuses onto silicon. On cooling down p-n junction get formed.

Depletion Region: Consider two types of doped semiconductors (p-type and n-type) in which p-type semiconductor contains negative acceptor ions and positively charged holes whereas n-type semiconductor contains positive donor ions and free electrons. Now these two types of semiconductors are joined together through some suitable technique to form p-n junction diode as shown in figure 19.1.

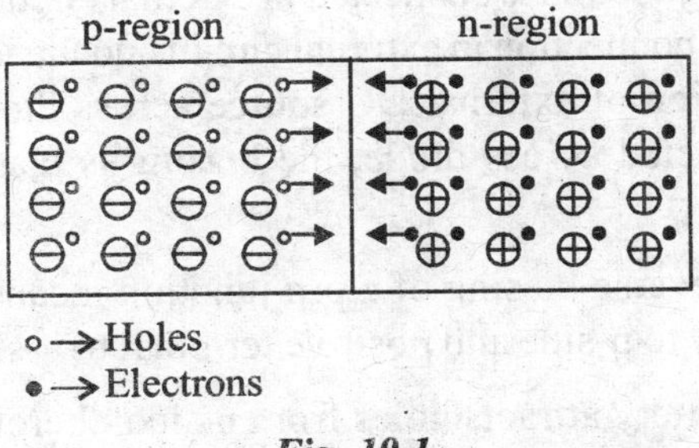

Fig. 19.1

The p-region has large concentration of holes (electrons are in minority) and n-region contains large number. of electrons (holes are minority carriers). Due to sudden difference in concentration at the junction, there is a tendency for the free electrons to diffuse (move) towards p-region and holes to n-region. Movement of electrons and holes due to difference in concentration is called diffusion process (Figure 19.1). As the free electrons move across the junction towards the p-region, donor atoms aquires positive charge. Positive ions so formed are very heavy and almost immobile, therefore, they are called immobile positive ions. After crossing the junction, free electrons falls into holes created by acceptor atoms.

Accepter atoms aquire negative charge after accepting free electron and a layer of negative ions establishes towards p-side of the junction. When sufficient number of positive and negative ions are formed, further diffusion is prevented. Now positive ions on n-side repel holes of p side and negative ions of p-side repel free electrons of n side. Thus, a barrier is established against further movement of holes and free electrons.

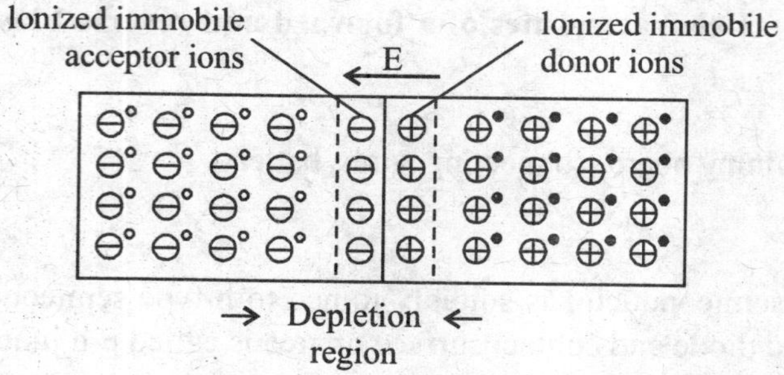

Fig. 19.2

This barrier is called potential barrier. A narrow region near the junction contains positive and negative ions. Since in this region donor atoms are depleted of electrons and acceptor atoms are depleted of holes, therefore, it is called depletion region or space charge region (Figure 19.2).

p-n Junction as a Rectifier & Biasing: The formation of depletion region in a p-n junction has a very importance use, that, this region allows flow of current only in one direction and block the current in other direction. That is why a p-n junction is widely used to obtain current in one direction i.e. as rectifier.

For rectification, the p-n junction is connected in external circuit and the junction diode is put in a suitable bias. Biasing means connection in external circuit and the junction diode is put in a suitable bias. Biasing means connection of external DC source across diode terminals. Depending upon polarity of DC source connected across diode, the biasing is classified in two manner, reverse biasing and forward biasing.

1. Reverse Biasing: Reverse biasing of a p-n junction means connecting negative terminal of external DC biasing battery to p-side and positive terminal to n-side of p-n junction.

Negative terminal of battery attracts holes from p-side, therefore, hole move away from the junction. Similarly, positive terminal of battery attracts electrons from n-side. Since the number of holes and free electrons decreases in the depletion region, therefore, thickness of depletion layer increases. The greater the reverse bias, the wider the depletion layer becomes.

Since barrier increases, therefore, majority carriers (holes in p-side and electrons in n-side) couldn't cross junction. As a result, the current due to majority charge carriers will be zero. This is called reverse biasing of p-n junction. However, a small current (in μA) flows due to minority charge carriers but effectively we have no current in reverse bias. The diode offers a high value of resistance in reverse bias.

2. Forward Biasing: When positive terminal of external biasing battery is connected to p-side of diode and negative terminal to the n-side of diode, the p-n junction diode is said to be the forward biased.

Negative terminal of battery repels electrons of n-side towards the junction, therefore they move into depletion region and merged with the positive ions and reconverts positive ions into neutral donor atoms. Similarly, holes are repelled by positive terminal of battery and they merged with negative ions and neutralize them. In this situation majority charge carriers cross the junction and give rise to a large amount of current which is called forward current. In such type of biasing the junction offers a low resistance.

So, from these two type of biasing we can conclude that only in forward bias we can get current from p-n junction diode. That is why, the p-n junction diode is used in rectifier, to convert AC into DC.

Volt-Ampere Characteristics: A p-n junction diode is symbolized as shown in fig. 19.3, where triangular shape refers to p-side of diode and straight vertical line refers to n-side of diode.

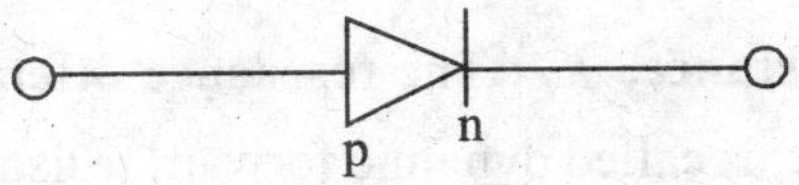

Fig. 19.3 : p-n junction diode

Forward Region: When p-n junction is in forward bias, the depletion region decreases. Ideally, diode should offer zero resistance and give rise to a large amount of current as shown in figure 19.4(a). But in practical diode no appreciable current flow till forward voltage is equal to knee potential (V_r). As the forward voltage is equal to knee voltage, the depletion layer completely disappears and current due to majority carriers rises exponentially as shown in figure 19.4(b).

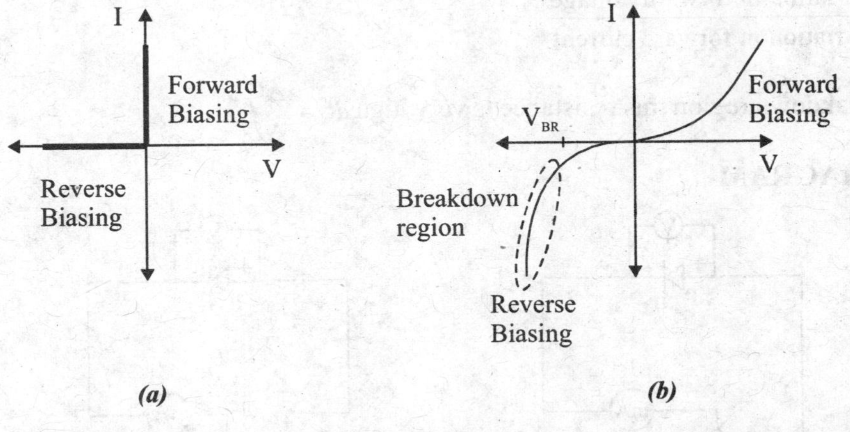

Figure 19.4 (a) V-I characteristic for on ideal diode, (b) V-I characteristic for a practical diode

Reverse Region : When p-n junction is reverse biased, movement of majority carries are opposed. Although minority carries can easily move and cross the junction and give riese to minority current which is very small concentration of these minority charge carries is independet of reverse voltage. Therefore, a constant reverse current flow as shown in fig. 19.4(b) for practical diodes. However, for ideal diode there should not any current in reverse bias as shonw in fig. (19.4).

When the reverse applied potential goes beyond a certain voltage V_{BR}, then current in reverse bias increases abruptly due to breakdown. So in this region, normal diodes destroy permanently and can not be used further. However this region has its important application, and some diode are made to use in this region is called zener diode.

Diode Resistance: According to ohm's law, voltage and current are proportional and there is always a straight line between voltage and current. The conductor or devices which follow ohm's law, called ohmic conductors or ohmic deivces.

According to the characteristic of p-n diode it is clear from the fig 19.4(b), that the ohm's law does not remain valid, that is way, the diodes are called nonohmic devices. However diode offers dynamic resistance.

(a) Dynamic forward resistance, R_f **:** The resistance offered by diode in forward region due to applied variation of voltage, is called dynamic forward resistance R_f

$$R_f = \frac{\text{variation in forward voltage}}{\text{variation in forward current}}$$

The value of forward resistance R_f is very low (a few ohms).

(b) Dynamic reverse resistance, R_r **:** The resistance offered by diode in reverse region due to applied variation of voltage in reverse direction is called dynamic reverse resistance R_r.

$$R_r = \frac{\text{variation in forward voltage}}{\text{variation in forward current}}$$

Upto breakdown region this resistance is very high $R_r = \frac{\Delta V_r}{\Delta I_r}$.

CIRCUIT DIAGRAM

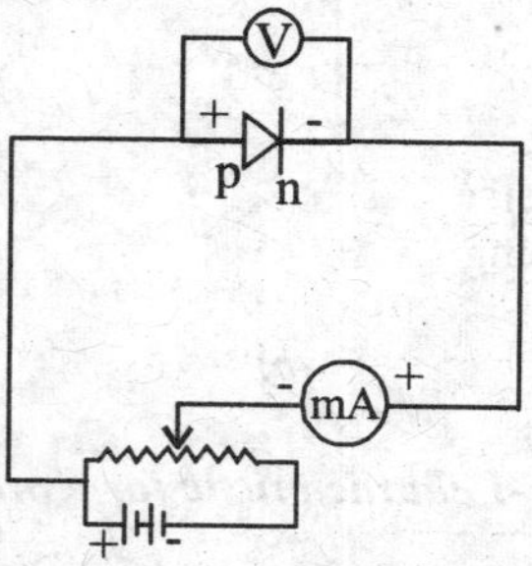

Fig. 19.5(a) Forward biased

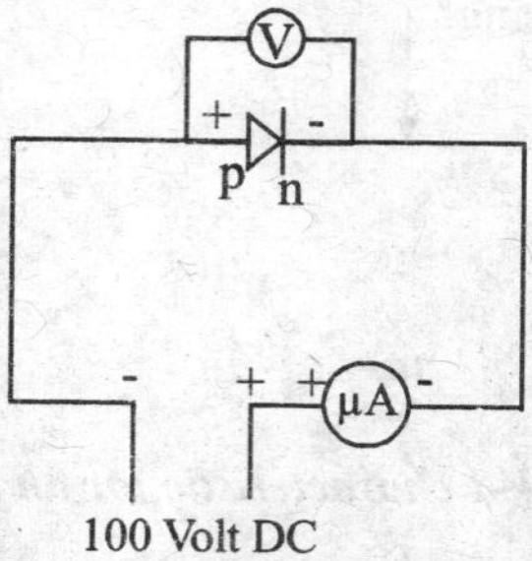

Fig. 19.5(b) Reverse biased

PROCEDURE

Forward Bias Characteristics

1. Assemble the circuit of figure 19.5(a) keep the 0-10V supply output at minimum position.
2. Switch ON the supply to the board. Slowly increase the 0-1-V supply and take readings of diode current at various voltage settings upto about 1.5 volt or less.
3. Plot the voltage current readings on a graph paper by taking voltage on the X-aixs and current on the Y-axis. The plot will look like the forward bias characteristics shown in figure 19.4(b).
4. We observe from the above characteristics that a forward voltage of about 0.2 volt is required before the diode start conduction.

Reverse Bias Characteristics

5. Now switch off the supply to the ETB and reverse the connection to the diode as per figure 19.5(b) and switch the current meter to μA range. Switch ON the supply to the unit and slowly increase the 0-10V supply. Note down the reading of current meter for various voltage setting upto 10 volt.
6. Plot the above readings on the same graph sheet by extending the X and Y axis on the negative side. The plot will look the one shown as reverse bias characteristics in figure 19.4(b).
7. We observe that very little reverse current called leakage current flows through the diode in the reverse bias mode. For the diode this leakage current will vary from piece to piece and will be upto around 2.8 μA maximum. This leakage current is too little for silicon signal diodes.

OBSERVATIONS

Table 1: For Forward Bias

S. No.	*Forward Voltage (V) (Range – IV)*	*Forward Current I (mA)*
1.		
2.		
3.		
4.		
5.		
6.		
7.		
8.		
9.		

Table 2: For Reverse Bias

S. No.	Reverse Voltage (V) (Range – 10V)	Reverse Current I (μA)
1.		
2.		
3.		
4.		
5.		
6.		
7.		

RESULT

1. The graph for the forward and the reverse bias characteristics of a germanium semiconductor diode has been plotted.
2. For germanim semiconductor diode

Forward resistance $R_f = \frac{\Delta V}{\Delta I} = ...\Omega$

Reverse resistance $R_r = \frac{\Delta V}{\Delta I} = ...\Omega$

PRECAUTIONS

1. The connection should be made carefully.
2. Apparatus should not be kept ON for a long time
3. The reading should be taken precisely.
4. In reverse biased the applied voltage should no be greater that rated voltage otherwise it may damage the diode.
5. The voltage should be get changed from the least value in forward biased.

VIVA-VOCE

Q. 1 What are semiconductors?

Ans. Semiconductors are those materials whose resistivity lies between those of conductors and insulator, i.e. of the order of 10^8 to 10^{-1} of units of ohm-meter.

Q. 2 What is forbidden energy gap?

Ans. In solids there is a gap between the valence band and the conduction band which does not contain any allowed energy levels. Hence this gap is known as forbidden energy gap.

Band gap of some semiconductors at room temperature.

Material	Band gap (e V)
Ge	0.66
Si	1.12
GaAs	1.43

Q. 3 On what factors does the reverse current depend in reverse bias arrangement?

Ans. The current in reverse bias arrangement depends on the temperature of the p-n junction and the energy band gap.

Q. 4 In which bias arrangement is the diode resistance high?

Ans. The resistance of p-n junction diode is very high in reverse bias arrangement.

Q. 5 What is a p-n junction?

Ans. A junction diode consists of a p-type crystal joined to an n-type so that they form one continuous crystal structures. The junction joining the two forms is called a p-n junction.

Q. 6 What is meant by forward biasing the diode?

Ans. When positive end of the battery (or supply) is connected to the p-type crystal and negative end to the n-type crystal, then diode is said to be in forward biasing.

□□□

EXPERIMENT 20

AIM

To determine the frequency of A.C. mains by an electromagnet by using a sonometer.

APPARATUS

Sonometer with steel wire of diameter of about 0.7 mm, electromagnet with A.C. supply step down transformer, kilogram weight.

THEORY

A sonometer is an apparatus by which the transverse vibrations of string can be studied. It demonstrates the relationship between the frequency of sound produced by a plucked string and the tension, length and mass per unit length of the string. For small amplitude vibrations, the frequency is proportional to

(i) square root of the tension of the string.

(ii) reciprocal of the square root of linear density of the string.

(iii) reciprocal of length of string.

If a wire of length l cm and linear mass density m gram per cm is stretched over two bridges with a tension of T dynes and plucked, it will emit a note of frequency given by, $n = \frac{1}{2l}\sqrt{\frac{T}{m}}$

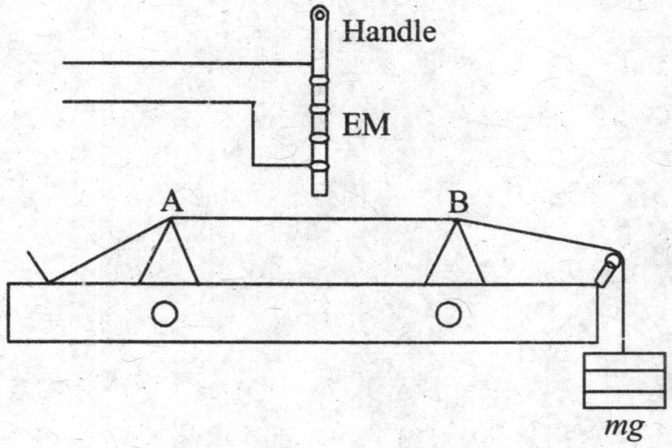

Fig. 20.1 Experiment arrangement

In this experiment the note emitted by the sonometer wire is tuned to the main hum by adjusting the tension and length until the wire is set in resonant vibrations by its attraction or repulsion by the electromagnet. As the wire is pulled by the electromagnet twice in each cycle one when its end-facing the wire is a north pole and again when it is a south pole, hence the frequency f of the A.C. main is half the frequency n of the vibrating string i.e. the frequency of A.C. mains,

$$f = \frac{n}{2}$$

Thus as T, l and m can be measured, n and hence f can be calculated. The value of m the mass per unit length can be determined by the method of weighing a definite length of the wire or by measuring the diameter with a screw gauge and assuming the density of steel to be 7.7 gm/cc.

WORKING FORMULA

The frequency of A.C. mains is given by

$$f = \frac{1}{4l}\sqrt{\frac{T}{m}}$$

where l is length of sonometer wire, T is Tension in sonometer wire, m is mass per unit length of sonometer wire.

PROCEDURE

1. Set up the appatatus as fig. 20.1 where AB is the sonometer wire, *mg* are the weights for alterning tension; EM is the electromagnet, A is the fixed wedge and B is the movable wedge.
2. Support the electromagnet in a retort stand and fix it between 8 and 10 cm from A and 2 to 3 mm above the wire.
3. Suspend a load of 1 kg and switch on the A.C. supply slide the wedge B gradually towards A until the wire starts vibrating. Make minor adjustements until the amptitude is maximum.
4. Record (i) the length of the vibrating wire AB and (ii) the value of the weight *mg* up to 3 kg in steps of half kg.
5. Measure the diameter of the wire by screw gauge. Find the mass per unit length from the given density of the wire.

OBSERVATIONS

Least count of screw gauge = ... cm.

Zero correction = ... cm.

Diameter of the wire, d_1 = ... cm, d_2 =.................. cm, d_3.................. cm.

Mean diameter of the wire, $r = d/2$ = ... cm.

Density of the wiere, ρ = ... gm/c.c (given)

Mass per unit length of the sonometer wire, $m = \pi r^2 \rho$ .... gm/cm.

Table 1: Determination of frequency of A.C. mains.

S. No.	*Stretching Load (M) gm*	*Length AB l(cm)*	$T = M \times 980$ *(dynes)*	$f = \frac{1}{4l}\sqrt{\frac{T}{m}}$
1.				
2.				
3.				
4.				
5.				

CALCULATIONS

Mean frequency of the A.C. mains = ... Hz.

RESULT

The frequency of A.C. supply = ... Hz

Standard value of frequency = ... Hz

Percentage error = ...%

PRECAUTIONS AND SOURCES OF ERROR

1. The pully should be frictionless
2. Wire should be uniform.
3. The nodes and loops should be sharply defined.

VIVA VOCE

Q. 1 What is A.C.?

Ans. In alternating current the movement of electric charge periodically reverses direction. Generally, AC refers to the form in which electricity is delivered to business and residences.

Q. 2 What is an electromagnet?

Ans. An electromagnet is a type of magnet in which the magnetic filed is produced by the flow of electric current. The magnetic field disappears when the current ceases.

Q. 3 On what factors does the frequency depend?

Ans. It depends on tension of the string, linear density of the string and length of the string.

Q. 4 What is sonometer? Name any instrument working on the same principle used in everyday life?

Ans. Sonometer is device used to find out the frequency of tuning fork. It work on the principle of resonance of vibration. It consist of hollow sounding box having two movable bridges. One end of string is fixed to the peg and second end passes over a pully fixed at other end of box and carries a hanger on which slotted weight can be a slipped.

The instruments we use on some principles are guitar, piano, etc.

Q. 5 What is resonance?

Ans. Resonance is the tendency of the system to oscillate or vibrate at larger amplitude at some frequency than at others.

Q. 6 Why the sound become loud when the stem of the tuning fork is pressed on the board?

Ans. When the stem of the vibrating tunning fork is pressed on boarti, a loud sound heared because the wire in tension vibrate with it producing sound effect. The sound become loud showing thereby that we are near resonating point.

Q. 7 What are nodes & antinodes?

Ans. **Nodes:** The fixed point in vibration where the amplitude is zero but the strain is maximum are called nodes.

Antinodes: The fixed point in vibration where the strain is least but amplitude is, maximum are called antinodes.

Q. 8 How would you locate nodes & antinodes in turning fork?

Ans. In tuning fork, free end acts as antinodes & middle point as the nodes. so now change will happen.

Q. 9 If the frequency of the string differs slightly from the frequency of tuning fork. What will happen?

Ans. Whey the frequency of the string differs lightly from the frequency of tuning fork loud sound is heared showing therely that we are near resonant point.

Q. 10 Why does rider fall down when the frequency of vibration of wire is equal to that of the tuning fork?

Ans. When the frequency of vibration of wire is equal to that of the tuning fork, the position of rider become antinode, so it falls down.

Q. 11 Can you test the position of resonance without using rider by?

Ans. Yes, the position of resonance can be tested without using rider by using beat method the vibrating tunning fork is moved along a were slowly till a loud sound is heared showing therely that we are near resonance point. Movable knife edge is now moved to this point. Again struck the fork & pluck the wire in middle. Again nodes produce will be slightly different, the movable arm is adjusted so that no beat is heared. The length between the two knife edge is noted.

Q. 12 For finding the fundamental frequency, why should we start with minimum distance between the wedges?

Ans. Since rider will fall at antinode, the first antinode will tell the fundamental frequency, so we start with minimum frequency.

❑❑❑

EXPERIMENT 21

AIM

To determine the band gap of Ge crystal by four probe method.

APPARATUS

Four probe arrangement, sample, oven, and thermometer.

THEORY

The four probe method is one of the standard and most widely used methods for the measurement of band gap of semiconductors. In its useful form, the four probes are collinear. The error due to contact resistance, which is significant in the electrical measurement on semiconductors, is avoided by the use of two extra contacts (probes) between the current contacts. In this arrangement the contact resistance may all be high compare to the sample resistance, but as long as the resistance of the sample and contact resistance's are small compared with the effective resistance of the voltage measuring device (potentiometer, electrometer or electronic voltmeter), the measured value will remain unaffected. Because of pressure contacts, the arrangement is also specially useful for quick measurement on different samples or sampling different parts of the sample.

Description of the experimental set-up

The experimental setup is shown in Fig. 21.1

(i) **Probes arrangement:** It has four individually spring loaded probes. The probes are collinear and equally spaced. The probes are mounted in a teflon bush, which ensure a good electrical insulation between the probes. A teflon spacer near the tips is also provided to keep the probes at equal distance. The probe arrangement is mounted in a suitable stand which also holds the sample plate. To ensure the correct measurement of sample temperature, the RTD is enbeded in the sample plate just below the sample. This stand also serves as the lid of temperature controlled oven. Proper leads are provided for the current and voltage measurement.

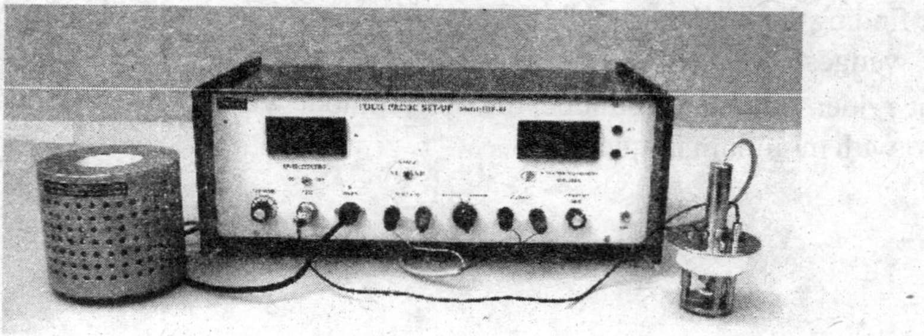

Fig. 21.1 Experimental setup

(ii) Sample: Germanium crystal in the form of a chip.

(iii) Oven: This is high quality temperature controlled oven suitable for four probe set-up. The oven has been designed for fast heating and cooling rates, which enhances the effectiveness of the controller.

(iv) Four probe setup (DEP-03): The set-up consists of three units housed in the same cabinet.

(a) **Oven controller:** Platinum RTD has been used for sensing the temperature. A wheatstone bridge and an instrumentation amplifier are used for signal conditioning. Feedback circuit ensures offset and linearity trimming and a fast accurate control of the oven temperature.

(b) **Multi-range digital voltmeter:** In this unit, intersil 3½ digit single chip A/D converter ICL 7107 has been used. It has accuracy, auto zero to less than 10 μV, zero drift-less than 1 μV/ °C, input bias current of 10 pA and roll over error of less than one count. Since the use of internal reference causes the degradation in performance due to internal heating, an external reference has been used.

(c) **Constant current generator:** It is an IC regulated current generator to provide a constant current to the outer probes irrespective of the changing resistance of the sample due to change in temperatures. The basic scheme is to use the feedback principle to limit the load current of the supply to preset maximum value. Variations in the current are achieved by a potentiometer included for that purpose. The supply is a highly regulated and practically ripple free d.c. source. The current is measured by the digital panel meter.

The dimensions of the germanium crystal are as follows:

Distance between the probes, $s = 2.0$ mm.

Thickness of the crystal, $W = 0.066$ cm.

We know that, $$\rho_0 = \frac{V}{I} 2\pi s = 1.256 \frac{V}{I} \qquad \text{...(21.1)}$$

Since the thickness of the crystal is very small compared to the probe distance, a correction factor for it has to be applied. In the present case the bottom surface is non-conducting so the correction factor for it would be

$$\rho = \frac{\rho_0}{f_7\left(\frac{W}{s}\right)} \qquad \text{...(21.2)}$$

The correction factor corresponding to $f_7\left(\frac{W}{s}\right)$ is 4.159. Therefore

$$\rho = \frac{\rho_0}{4.159} \qquad \text{...(21.3)}$$

From equations (21.2) and (21.3), we obtain

$$\rho = \frac{V \times 1.256}{I \times 4.159} = \frac{0.3020 \times V}{I} \quad ...(21.4)$$

The bandgap of semiconductor crystal is given by

$$E_g = 2k \frac{\log_e \rho}{(1/T)} \quad ...(21.5)$$

where k is Boltzmann constant and T is temperature in Kelvin.

Plot a graph between $\log_{10} \rho$ versus $\frac{1}{T} \times 10^3$ (Fig. 21.2). Find the slope of the curve given by

$$E_g = 2k \frac{2.3026 \times \log_{10} \rho}{(10^3 / T)} \text{ eV}$$

Putting this value of curve slope in equation (21.5), we obtain

$$E_g = 2 \times 8.6 \times 10^{-5} \times \frac{2.3026 \times \log_{10} \rho}{(10^3 / T)} \text{ eV.}$$

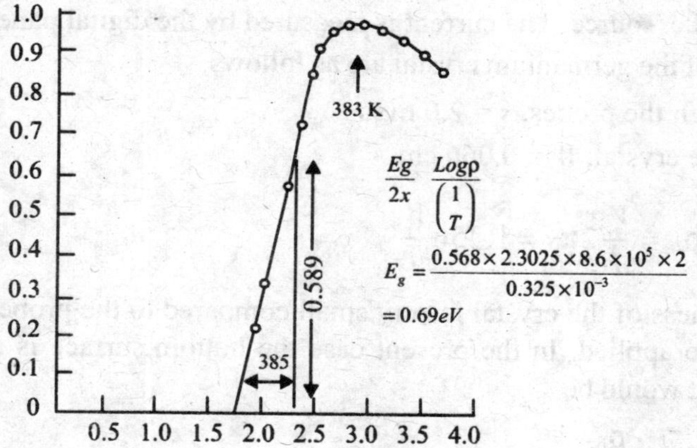

Fig. 21.2 The resistivity of a Germinium cystal as a function of invense temperature

WORKING FORMULA

The energy band gap for germanium crystal (Ge) is

$$E_g = 2k \frac{\log_e \rho}{(1/T)}$$

where k is Boltzmann constant, T is temperature in kelvin and ρ is resistivity.

PROCEDURE

1. First take out the four probe arrangement and put it on a plane surface. Now put the sample on the circular base plate of the four probe arrangement so that the bottom surface non-conducting and four probes are in the middle of the crystal. Apply some pressure slightly on the pipe so that it clearly makes the contacts with the sample and tighten the screw. Check the continuity between the four probes with the sample by the multimeter. If the contacts are loose tighten the three screw provided on the top of the base plate. The resistance between the green and red pairs of leads must nearly be of the order of 2 to 4 kΩ. Put the four probe arrangement to measure the oven temperatures.
2. Connect the outer pair of probes (green pair) to the constant current source marked current and the inner pair of probes (red pair) to the voltage source marked voltage.
3. Connect the setup with the mains and switch it ON.
4. Put the selector switch in voltage position and range multiplier switch at "1" position. Adjust zero with the help of ZERO ADJ keeping either the current terminals in open or the voltage terminal short.
5. Change the selector switch in current position and apply some current say 2 to 3 mA constant for whole set of readings and note this value of current. Change the selector switch in voltage position with range switch at 10 position and note the corresponding voltage and temperature. Record these readings in table.
6. Put the oven switch at L position. Connect the oven with the oven supply and switch ON. A glowing LED will show the ON position of the supply. Measure the voltage at different values of temperature keeping the current constant. Maximum value of temperature should not be more than 100°C. Record these readings.
7. Plot a graph between the resistivity ($\log_{10}\rho$) and inverse of temperature ($10^3/T$). Find the slope of the curve and put the value of $\log_{10}\rho/(1/T)$ in the energy band gap formula.

OBSERVATIONS

Current I = ... mA.

Table 1: Determination of resistivity and temperature

S. No.	*Temperature T (°C)*	*Voltage V (Volt)*	*Temperature (Volt)*	*ρ (ohm-cm)*	*$10^3/T$*	*$\log_{10}\rho$*
1.						
2.						
3.						
4.						
5.						
6.						

CALCULATIONS

Plot a graph between $\log_{10}\rho$ versus $\frac{1}{T}\times 10^3$ and find the slope of the curve. The band gap for germanium crystal is

$$E_g = 2\times 8.6\times 10^{-5}\times \frac{2.3026\times \log_{10}\rho}{(10^3/T)} = ...\text{eV}.$$

RESULT

The graph shows the variation of resistivity of the given (Ge) sample with temperature.
The experimentally observed value of E_g = ... eV.
Standard value of E_g = 0.67 eV.
Percentage error = ... %.

PRECAUTIONS AND SOURCES OF ERROR

1. Zero adjustment of current and voltage should be made properly at the initial stage.
2. The four probes and the surface on which the probes are placed should have proper contact.
3. Reading of voltage and temperature must be taken simultaneously.
4. The area of the point of contact between metallic probes and the semiconductor crystal chip should small compared to the distance between the probes.
5. The current should remain constant throughout the experiment.
6. Temperature should not cross 100°C, otherwise crystal will damage.

VIVA VOCE

Q.1 What are semiconductors?

Ans. Semiconductors are those materials whose resistivity lies between .those of conductor and insulator, i.e. of the order of 10^8 to 10^{-1} of the units of ohm-meter

Q.2 What is forbidden energy gap?

Ans. In solids there is a gap between the valence band and the conduction band which does not contain any allowed energy levels. Hence this gap is known as forbidden energy gap.

Q.3 What are holes?

Ans. Holes act as carriers of positive charge in valence band whose displacement is in a direction opposite to that of electrons.

Q.4 What are intrinsic and extrinsic semiconducrtors?

Ans. When the semiconductor is in pure state it is known as intrinsic semiconductors. When some limited quantity of suitable impurity is mixed in pure semiconductors the resulting semiconductor is known as extrinsic semiconductors.

Q.5 What are n-type and p-type semiconductors?

Ans. When some atoms of pentavalent element like As, Sb etc. are mixed as impurity with pure semiconductor, the resulting semiconductor is known as n-type semiconductor and when some atoms of trivalent element like Ga, Al, In etc. are mixed as impurity with pure semiconductor the resulting semiconductor is known as p-type semiconductor.

Q.6 Which type of impurities are added in n-type semiconductor?

Ans. Impurities from group V elements e.g. Arsenic and Antimony are added in n-type semiconductor.

Q.7 Which type of impurities are added in p-type semiconductor?

Ans. Impurities from group III elements e.g. Boron, Aluminium are added in p-type semiconductor.

Q.8 What are the majority charge carriers in p-type semiconductor?

Ans. Majority charge carriers in p-type semiconductor are holes.

Q.9 What are the majority charge carriers in n-type semiconductor?

Ans. Majority charge carriers in n-type semiconductor are electrons.

Q.10 What do you mean by Fermi level?

Ans. The Fermi energy is the highest occupied state in a system of fermions at aboultc zero temperature. It is the energy level at which the probability of occupation by an electron is exactly one half at room temperature.

Q.11 What is the positions of Fermi level in p-type and n-type semi conductor with respect to the positions of conduction and valence bands?

Ans. If we introduce donor or acceptor level into the intrinsic semiconductor, the Fermi level will change. In an n type semiconductor the level will usually lie between donor level and conduction band and for a p-type semiconductor, it will lie between the valance band and acceptor level.

Q.12 Why a semiconductor behaves as an insulator at 0° K?

Ans. In semiconductors, some thermal energy is required for electrons in valence band to cross the energy band gap and reach to conduction band. At 0° K this sufficient energy is not available for electrons to jump from VB to CB and leads to conduction. Thus semiconductor behaves as an insulator at 0° K.

Q.13 Why the resistivity.of a semiconductor decreases with increasing temperature?

Ans. As the temperature increases from 0° K an increase in the number of valence electrons absorbed sufficient thermal energy to beak the covalent bond and contribute to the number of the charge carries this leads to decrease in resistivity.

Q.14 What are the energy band gap of diamond, silicon, germanium, grey tin and lead?

Ans. Diamond $E_g = 5.4eV$

Silicon $E_g = 1.1eV$,

Germanium $E_g = 0.72\,eV$,

Grey tin $E_g = 0.08\,eV$,

Lead $E_g = 0$

Q.15 Distinguish between diffusion current and generation current in a semi-conductor.

Ans. The diffusion current (I_{diff}) refers to the movement of majority carrers. Majority carries consist of electrons (in the conduction band) that travel from the *n* to the *p* side and hole (vacancies in the valence band) that travel form the *p* to the *n* side. Whereas the drift current (Idrift) refers to the movement of minority carries across the *pn* junction. The minority carriers also consist of electrons and holes yet the direction of their movement is opposite that of majority carries.

Q.16 On what factors does the reverse current depend in reverse bias arrangement?

Ans. The current in reverse bias arrangement depends on the temperature of the pn junction and the energy band gap.

Q.17 In which bias arrangement is the diode resistance high?

Ans. The resistance of pn junction diode is very high in reverse bias arrangement.

Q.18 What is a pn junction?

Ans. A junction diode consists of a type crystal joined to an n-type so that they form one continuous crystal structures. The junction joining the two forms is called a pn junction.

Q.19 What is meant by forward biasing the diode?

Ans. When positive end of the battery (or supply) is connected to the p-type crystal and negative end to the n-type crystal, then diode is said to be in forward biasing.

❑❑❑

EXPERIMENT 22

AIM

To draw VI characteristics of a photocell and to verify the inverse square law of radiation.

APPARATUS

Photocell kit, incandescent lamp, a photocell, connecting wires, metre scale etc.

THEORY

The photo electric emission may regarded as a phenomenon of liberation of an electron at the surface of a metal when a photon of light impinges, on a metallic surface and transfers enough energy to the electron to escape through the potential barier layer. There are basically four forms: photoemissive type, photovoltaic type, photo conductive junction type, and photo conductive bulk effect type.

We shall consider only the photo voltic type. The photo voltaic effect can be considered as the generation of a voltage across a circuit element under illumination.

Photovoltaic Effect: When a light of some particular frequency or intensity falls on a semiconductor then a potential difference developes between the ends of semiconductor material. This generation of voltage or potential difference due to incident light photons is called photovoltaic effect. The device based on this effect is callcd photovoltaic cell.

When light falls on the semiconductor then charge carriers accumulate and give rise to potential difference. The potential difference depends on charge carriers, consequently on the intensity of incident radiation. The photovoltaic cell consists of semiconductor like germanium, silicon etc. with a metal plate. The circuit symbol of a photovoltaic cell is given in figure 22.1.

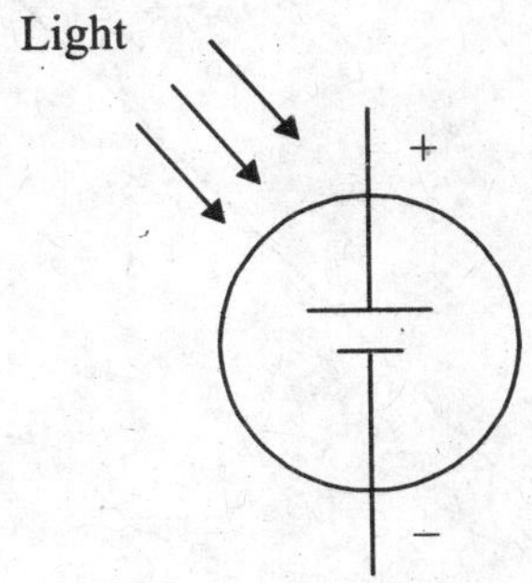

Fig. 22.1 Circuit symbol

Generally, selenium and silicon are used for the manufacture of these types of photo cells.

Construction of Selenium Photocell: The selenium photocell, just like the selenium rectifier consists of a base plate which may be of aluminium, steel or brass depending upon the method of manufacturer. On this plate a very thin layer of special grade selenium is deposited followed by a deposition of cadmuim or cadmium oxide.

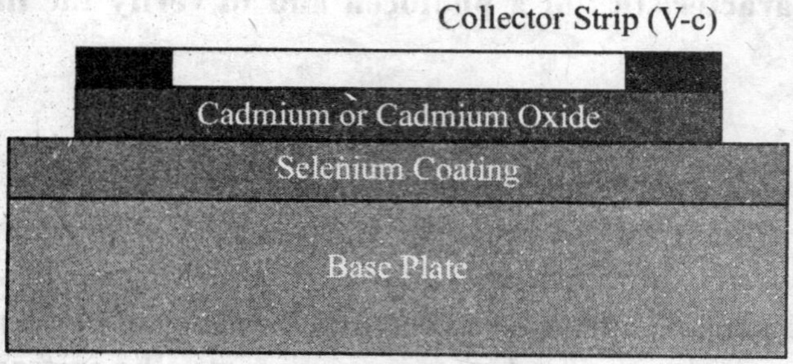

Fig. 22.2 Construmtion of selenium photocell

Inverse square law: If L is the luminous intensity of a light source and E is the intensity of illumination at a point distant r from it, then according to inverse square law

$$E = L/r^2.$$

If this light is allowed to fall on a photocell then the current I measured using a micro-ammeter is proportional to intensity of illumination E given by

$$E = L/r^2 = kI$$

where k is a constant.

Hence a graph between $1/r^2$ and I is a straight line as shown in Fig. 22.3, which verifies inverse square law of radiation.

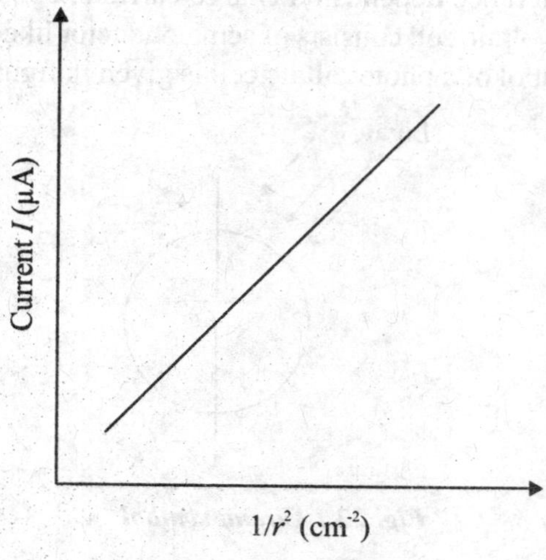

Fig. 22.3 I versus $1/r^2$

CIRCUIT DIAGRAM

The circuit diagram is shown in Fig. 22.4

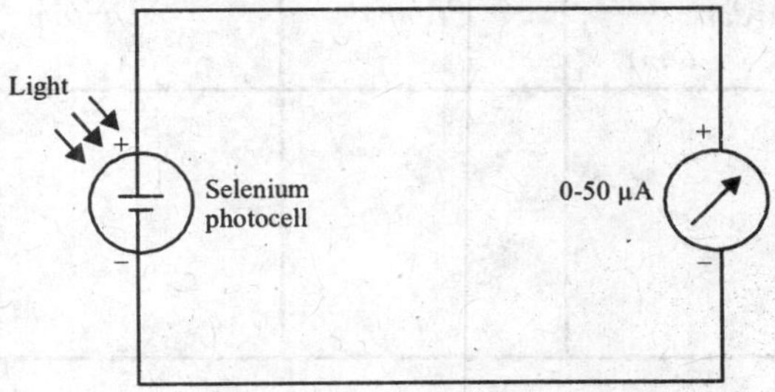

Fig. 22.4 Circuit diagram

PROCEDURE

1. Align the incandescent lamp source and the photocell housing along a straight line.
2. Set the photocell at a distance of 20 cm from the source.
3. Make the connections as shown in Fig. 22.4.
4. Switch on the lamp. The light from the lamp should fall on the aperture of the photocell housing directly.
5. Keeping the distance and aperture of photocell constant, gradually increase the voltage across the photocell starting from zero, note down the current.
6. Plot a graph for voltage (volts) along the X-axis and the current (μA) along the Y-axis. The current saturates at certain voltage (say V_{sat}).
7. Now keeping the voltage at saturation voltage, adjust the variable aperture till a considerable current is registered on the micro-ammeter.
8. Keep the voltage and aperture fixed and record the photocell current readings at distances 5 cm apart till the current is nearly zero. Note down the distances also.
9. Plot a graph for $1/(\text{distance})^2$ along the X-axis and corresponding current along Y-axis. The graph will be a straight line.

OBSERVATIONS

Table 1: Characteristics of photocell

S. No.	*Voltage V (Volts)*	*Current I (mA)*
1.		
2.		
3.		
4.		
5.		

Table 2: Verification of inverse square law

Potential difference across the photoelectric cell, V_{sat} = ...Volt.

S. No.	Distance between lamp and photocell r (cm)	$r^2 (cm^2)$	$1/r^2 (cm^{-2})$	Current I (A)
1.				
2.				
3.				
4.				
5.				

RESULT

The graph shows the V-I characteristics of a photoelectric cell.

The graph between $1/r^2$ and I, a straight line verifies the inverse square law of radiation.

PRECAUTIONS AND SOURCES OF ERROR

1. The light from the lamp should fall normally on the photoelectric cell.
2. The distance r should be measured carefully.
3. The voltage should remain constant during inverse square law verification.
4. Light from any other source should not fall on the photocell.

VIVA VOCE

Q.1 What is photo voltaic effect?

Ans. When a light of same particular frequency or intensity falls on a semiconductor then a potential difference developes between the ends of semiconductor material. This genera- tion of voltage is called photovoltaic effect.

Q.2 What is photovoltaic cell?

Ans. The device depends on photovoltaic effect is called photovoltaic cell.

Q.3 On which factors potential difference produced in the photovoltaic effect depends?

Ans. It depends on charge carriers, and intensity of incident radiation.

Q.4 Give difference between photovoltaic cell and LED.

Ans. A photovoltaic cell generates its own electromotive force, when light incident on it, while LED is a diode that emits light when a current passes through it in forward direction.

Q.5 Give the circuit symbols of photovoltaic cell and LED?

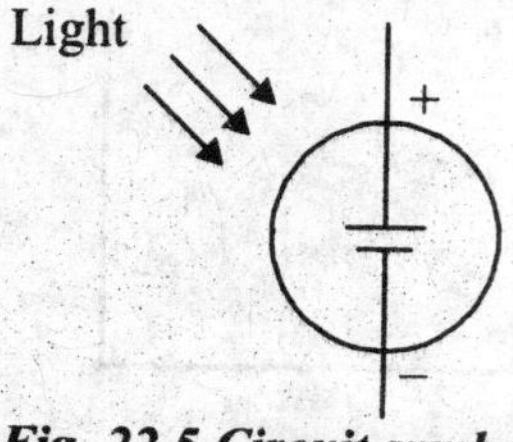

Fig. 22.5 Circuit symbol of photovoltaic cell

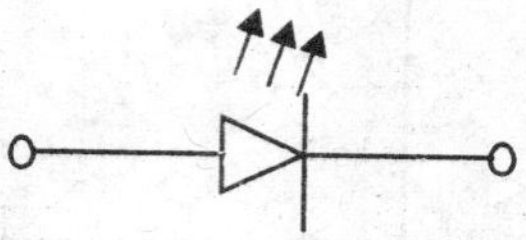

Fig. 22.6 Circuit symbol of LED

❑❑❑

EXPERIMENT 23

AIM

To determine the acceleration due to gravity (*g*) by Kater's reversible pendulum.

APPARATUS

Kater's pendulum, a telescope, a stop watch and a meter rod.

THEORY

Kater's pendulum is a compound pendulum constructed on the principle that centre of oscillation and centre of suspension are interchangeable. It consists of a brass or a steel bar capable of vibrating about two adjustable knife edges K_1 and K_2 facing each other. Two metal weights w_1 and w_2 can be made to slide, along the length of the bar and can be clamped in any position. Two wooden weights W_1 and W_2 exactly similar to the metal weights can also slide along the bar. The metal weights are placed between the two knife edges and the wooden weights are fixed symmetrically at the ends of the bar as shown in Fig. 23.1. In this position the centre of gravity lies in between and near one of the knife edges.

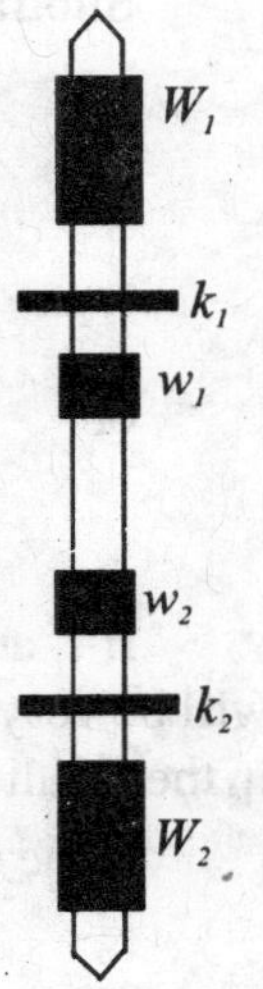

Fig. 23.1
Kater's pendulum

The position of the two knife edges and the weights W_1 and W_2 are so adjusted that the time periods of the pendulum about the two knife edges are equal. In such a case one knife edge is at the centre of oscillation with respect to the other and the distance between the two knife edges is equal to the length of an equivalent simple pendulum *L*. If *t* is the time period, then the acceleration due to gravity *g* can be found out from the relation

$$t = 2\pi\sqrt{\frac{L}{g}}$$

It is. however, very difficult and tedious to make the time of oscillation about the two knife edges exa ctly equal. Bassel showed that it was not absolutely necessary to make the time periods about two knife-edges exactly equal. The calculations of the value of *g* can be made if time periods were very nearly equal, the difference being not mote than 0.01 second.

If t_1 and t_2 are time periods about the two knife edges K_1 and K_2 respectively and l_1 is the length of the knife edge K_1 and l_2 that of the knife edge K_2 from the centre of gravity, then

$$t_1 = 2\pi\sqrt{\frac{K^2 + l_1^2}{l_1 g}} \text{ and } t_2 = 2\pi\sqrt{\frac{K^2 + l_2^2}{l_2 g}}$$

or
$$t_1^2 l_1 = \frac{4\pi^2}{g}\left(K^2 + l_1^2\right) \quad ...(23.1)$$

and
$$t_2^2 l_2 = \frac{4\pi^2}{g}\left(K^2 + l_2^2\right) \quad ...(23.2)$$

Subtracting (23.2) from (23.1), we obtain

$$\frac{4\pi^2}{g} = \frac{t_1^2 l_1 - t_2^2}{(l_1 + l_2)(l_1 - l_2)} = \frac{t_1^2 + t_2^2}{2(l_1 - l_2)} + \frac{t_1^2 - t_2^2}{2(l_1 - l_2)}$$

or
$$g = \frac{8\pi^2}{\dfrac{t_1^2 + t_2^2}{l_1 + l_2} + \dfrac{t_1^2 - t_2^2}{l_1 - l_2}}$$

If t_1 and t_2 are very nearly equal and l_1 and l_2 differ by a fairly large amount the second term will be very small and hence if its value is determined with only a fair degree of accuracy, the error in the result will be practically negligible.

If the second term is negligible, then

$$\frac{4\pi^2}{g} = \frac{t_1^2 + t_2^2}{2(l_1 + l_2)} \text{ or } g = \frac{8\pi^2 (l_1 + l_2)}{t_1^2 + t_2^2}$$

If $t_1 = t_2$ then

$$\frac{4\pi^2}{g} = \frac{t^2}{(l_1 + l_2)}$$

or
$$g = \frac{4\pi^2 (l_1 + l_2)}{t^2}$$

Working Formula: The value of acceleration due to gravity is given by

or
$$g = \frac{4\pi^2 L}{t^2}$$

where L is the distance between the knife edges and t is the time period of oscillation.

PROCEDURE

1. Clamp the weight W_1 at one end of the pendulum and the knife edge K_1 a little below it as shown in Fig. 1.
2. Clamp the knife edge K_2 at the other end with small metal weights w_1 and w_2 in the middle of the pendulum and W_2 at the other end of the pendulum.
3. Measure the distance L between the knife edges with a meter scale.
4. Suspend the pendulum about K_1 at the rigid support fixed on the wall. Adjust the telescope to focus the pendulum sharply on the cross wire and note the time taken for 40 oscillations of small amplitude. Counting of time period should be started when the pendulum is passing through its equilibrium position.
5. Now suspend the pendulum about K_2 and measure time taken for 40 oscillations.
6. Move W_1 and W_2 slightly outwards and repeat the observations. If the difference in time periods increases by doing so, move the two weights in the opposite direction and repeat the observations.
7. Go on moving W_1 and W_2 in equal small steps till the time periods are very nearly same.
8. Now move W_1 and W_2 slightly to reduce time difference further till the difference is almost zero.
9. Repeat the observations for three more distances between the knife edges.

OBSERVATION TABLE

Table 1: Determination of *t*

Sr. No.	*Distance between knife edges, L (m)*	*Knife edge*	*Time for 40 oscillations (seconds)*	*Mean value of time period t = $(t_1+t_2)/2$ (seconds)*
1		K_1		
		K_2		
2		K_1		
		K_2		
3		K_1		
		K_2		

CALCULATIONS

First set: g_1 = ... m/s^2.
Second set: g_2 = ... m/s^2.
Third set: g_3 = ... m/s^2.
Mean value of g = ... m/s^2.

RESULT

Acceleration due to gravity in the laboratory = ... m/s^2.
Actual value of g = ... m/s^2.
% error = ... %

PRECAUTIONS AND SOURCES OF ERROR

1. The heavy weight should be placed at one end so that the C.G. lies near one of the knife-edges and wooden weight W' symmetrically at the other end to avoid error due to drag.
2. The two knife edges should be parallel to each other.
3. The amplitude of vibration should be small so that the motion of the pendulum satisfies the condition $\sin\theta = \theta$.
4. To avoid any irregularity of motion the time period should be noted after the pendulum has made a few vibrations and the vibrations have become regular.
5. For final observation the time of at least 100 vibrations must be taken with an accurate stop watch.
6. Slight error is introduced due to resistance of air, curvature of knife edges, yielding of support, and finite amplitude.

VIVA-VOCE

Q. 1. What do you mean by acceleration due to gravity?

Ans. The acceleration produced in the motion of a body under the effect of gravity is called acceleration due to gravity.

Q. 2. What is S.I. unit of acceleration due to gravity?

Ans. The S.I. unit of acceleration due to gravity is m/s^2.

Q. 3. How does the value of 'g' vary at different places and different distances from the surface of the earth?

Ans. The value of 'g' decreases with altitude and depth. It is maximum on the surface of earth. Its value at a place decrease with decrease in latitude of the place. The effect of earth's rotational motion is maximum at equator and zero at poles.

Q. 4. What is Kater's pendulum?

Ans. It is a compound pendulum based on the principle the centre of oscillation and centre of suspension are interchangeable.

Q. 5. What is simple harmonic oscillation? Does the Kater's pendulum undergo simple harmonic motion?

Ans. An oscillation in which the acceleration of particle is directly proportional to its displacement from a fixed point and is always directed towards the fixed point is called simple harmonic motion. Yes, Kater's pendulum undergoes simple harmonic motion.

Q. 6. Define centre of suspension and centre of oscillation.

Ans. The point through which the horizontal axis about which the pendulum vibrates, passes is called the center of suspension. The point at a distance equal to the length of an equivalent simple pendulum from the point of suspension on the straight line passing through the centre of gravity is called the centre of oscillation.

Q. 7. Why do you place the heavy masses near the knife edges?

Ans. By placing the heavy masses near the knife edges the centre of gravity lies in between and near one of the knife edges.

Q. 8. Is it necessary to have the two time periods exactly equal?

Ans. Yes, it is necessary that the two time periods should be equal, the difference being not more than 0.01 second.

Q. 9. How will you find the value of acceleration due to gravity if the two time periods are not exactly equal?

Ans. The two time periods are made equal by adjusting the position of wooden weights.

Q. 10. What is the use of wooden weights? Where these should be placed?

Ans. The wooden weights are used to make the two time periods equal. These should be placed at the ends of the steel bar.

Q. 11. Why telescopė is used to count the number of oscillations?

Ans. The amplitude of oscillations is kept very small; therefore telescope is used to count the number of oscillations.

Q. 12. What is the length of an equivalent simple pendulum?

Ans. When the two time periods are equal, then the distance between the two knife edges is equal to the length of equivalent simple pendulum. In such a case one knife edge is at the centre of oscillation and the other is at the centre of suspension.

❑❑❑

EXPERIMENT 24

AIM

To study the characteristic of photovoltaic (solar cell)

APPARATUS

The complete experimental set-up consists of the followings

One board built up of digital D.C. ammeter, digital D.C. voltmeter. digital DC voltmeter, socket for table lamp with intensity control solar cell mounted, table lamp 100 watt, five different area choppers.

THEORY

A solar cell is basically a pn junction which converts solar energy into electrical energy. The conversion of optical energy into electrical energy is known as photo voltalic effect. Hence a solar cell is called a photovolatic cell.

When a solar cell is illuminated the photons incident on the cell generate electron hole pairs. By diffusion in the material the electrons and holes reach the junction. At the junction the barrier field separates the positive and negative charge carriers. Under the action of the electric field, the electron (minority carriers) from p region arc swept into n region. Similarly, the holes from n region are swept into p region it leads to an increase in the number of holes on the p side and of electrons on the two junction. The accumulation of charges on the two sides of the junction produces an emf which is called a photo emf. The photo emf is known as the open circuit voltage. It is proportional to the illumination and the size of the illuminated area. When an external circuit is connected across the solar cell terminals the minority carriers return to their original sides throughout the external circuit, causing a current to flow through the circuit. Thus the solar cell behaves as a battery with n-side as the negative terminal and p-side as the positive terminal. The photo emf or voltage can be measured with a voltmeter. The process of genération of photovoltaic voltage is shown in figure 24.1

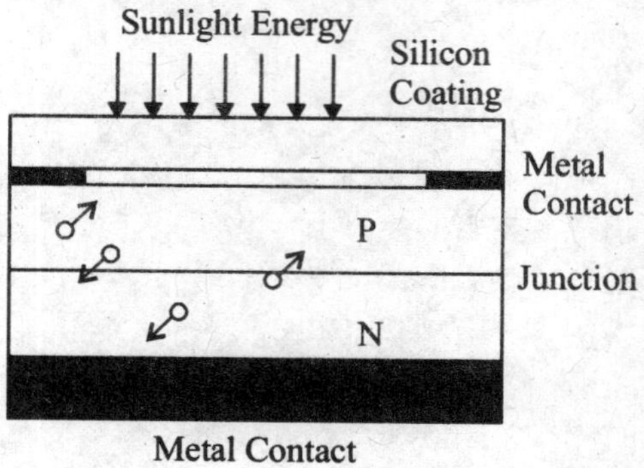

Fig. 24.1 Solar Cell

Mostly solar cells are fabricated from silicon single crystals. Silicon is not transparent for visible light Therefore, the surface layer of the cell, which is of p-type is made extremely then to enable maximum light to penetrate the junction. It is desired that the absorption of light takes place at the junction region such that the generated electron hole pairs can be separated by the junction region such that the generated electron-hole pairs can be separated by the junction field before they are lost by recombination. To enhance the transmission of light into the material an anti reflect ion coating is given over the p type layer. This metallic films vacuum deposited suitable on both, the sides of the cell act as electrodes. An open circuit voltage of peak value of 0.6V is generated by a solar cell. Silicon wafers of 1" dia to 4" dia arc used to fabricate solar cells in order to enhance the total voltage and current output, a number of pn junctions are formed on a wafer using a mesh type or finger like electrode structure. To increase power output, solar cells are arrayed into a series chain or parallel chain and are interconnected. Such an arrangement is called a solar panel. In normal use single solar cell is rarely used, as its output is very low.

The illumination characteristics of a solar cell panel are shown in figure 24.2. It is seen that the current through the solar cell increases as the intensity of light failing on the panel increases.

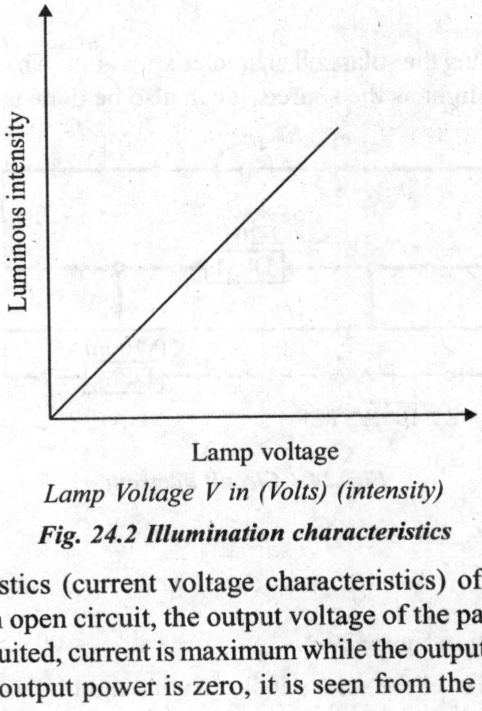

Lamp Voltage V in (Volts) (intensity)

Fig. 24.2 Illumination characteristics

The output characteristics (current voltage characteristics) of a solar panel are shown in figure 24.3. It is seen that on open circuit, the output voltage of the panel is 0.6V and the current is zero. If the panel is short circuited, current is maximum while the output voltage of the panel becomes zero. In both the cases, the output power is zero, it is seen from the curve that the voltage varies depending on the current drawn.

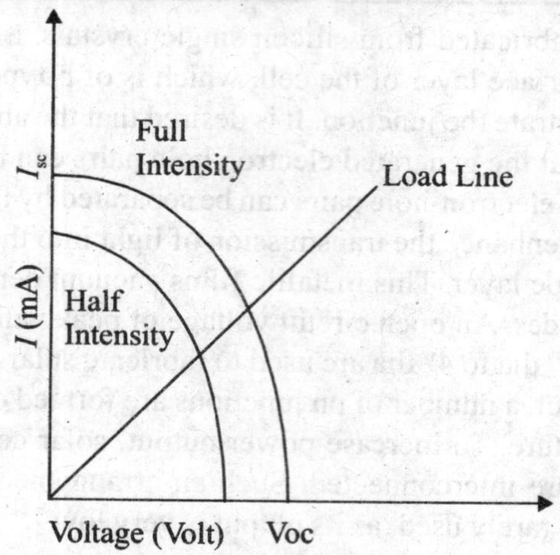

Fig. 24.3 V-I characteristics

CIRCUIT DIAGRAM

The circuit for determining the solar cell characteristics is shown in figure 24.4. The experiment is to be performed, using sunlight as the source. It can also be done using a 100 W lamp.

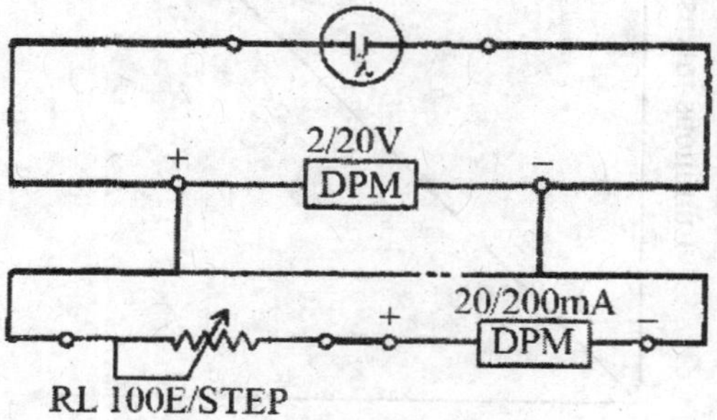

Fig. 24.4 Circuit diagram

PROCEDURE

Illumination Characteristics

1. Make the circuit as shown in figure 24.4.
2. A 100W lamp is arranged over the solar panel such that light falls on it at normal. The intensity control is kept at its minimum and lamp is switched on.
3. The load is kept at 0 ohms and the short circuit current is noted.
4. The intensity of the lamp is varied in steps and the current is noted at each setting.
5. A graph is drawn between the current and intensity (intensity is taken as proportional to the voltage given to the lamp and volts are taken as units on the x-axis in place of intensity).

V-I Characteristics

1. The intensity of the lamp is kept at the minimum. The load resistance is not connected into the circuit. The open circuit voltage is noted.
2. The output of the solar panel is shorted. The short circuit current is noted.
3. The load dial is set at 100 ohms. The voltage and current are noted down. The load is varied in steps upto 100 ohms and at each setting the voltage and current are recorded.
4. The intensity of the lamp is increased. At this setting the load is again from 100 to 900 ohms and the corresponding voltage and current are recorded. The open circuit voltage and short circuit current are also determined and recorded.
5. The intensity of the lamp is set to its maximum step 4 is repeated.
6. A graph for current versus voltage is drawn.

OBSERVATIONS

Table 1: Illumination Characteristics

R_L =........ohms

S.No.	*Intensity (DC volts)*	*Current (DC mA)*
1.		
2.		
3.		
4.		
5.		

Table 2: V-I Characteristics

S.No.	R_L	*Intensity* I_1 =		*Intensity* I_2 =		*Intensity* I_3 =	
	Ohms	*Voltage (V)*	*Current (mA)*	*Voltage (V)*	*Current (mA)*	*Voltage (V)*	*Current (mA)*
1.							
2.							
3.							
4.							
5.							
6.							
7.							
8.							
9.							
10.							

Open circuit voltage $(R_L = \infty)$ = ...volts for I_1

= ....volts for I_2

= ....volts for I_3

Short circuit current $(R_L = 0)$ = ...mA for I_1

= ....mA for I_2

= ....mA for I_3

PRECAUTIONS AND SOURCES OF ERROR

1. Light should fall normally on die solar cell.
2. The solar cell should not be exposed to light for a long time continuously.
3. The reading must take carefully.

VIVA VOCE

Q.1 What is photovoltaic effect?

Ans. When a light of same particular frequency (or intensity) falls on a semiconductor then a potential difference develops between the ends of semiconductor, material. This generation of voltage is called photovoltaic effect.

Q.2 What is photovoltaic cell?

Ans. The device based on photovoltaic effect is called photovoltaic cell.

Q.3 On which factors potential difference produced in the photovoltaic effect depends?

Ans. It depends on charge carriers and intensity of incident radiation.

Q.4 Give difference between photovoltaic cell and LED.

Ans. A photovoltaic cell generates its own electromotive force, when passes through it in forward direction.

Q.5 Give the circuit symbols of photovoltaic cell and LED?

Ans.

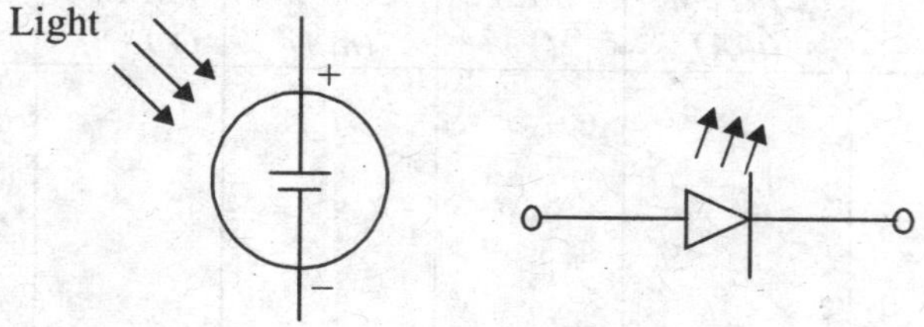

Fig. 1 *Fig. 2*

Q.6 Write down construction of photovoltaic cell.

Ans. The photovoltaic cell consists of semiconductor like Gec, Si etc with a metal plate.

□□□

TABLE OF CONSTANTS

1. Fundamental Physical Constants

A. Mechanics and classical physics:

Gravitational constant, $G = 6.67 \times 10^{-11}$ N m^2 kg^{-1}
Acceleration due to gravity, $g = 9.80$ m/s^2 = 32 ft/s^2
Speed of sound in dry air (stp), $v = 331$ m/s

B. Astronomical

Length of earth year = 3.16×10^7 sec
Radius of the earth = 6.38×10^6m = 3965 miles
Mean radius of the earth's orbit = 1.49×10^{11} m = 9.26×10^7 miles
Mass of the earth = 5.98×10^{24} kg
Weight of the earth = 3.3×10^{18} lb

C. Heat and kinetic theory

Avogadro constant $N_A = 6.02 \times 10^{26}$ kmole^{-1}
Boltzmann constant, $k = 1.38 \times 10^{-23}$ J K^{-1}
Universal gas constant, $R = 8310$ J kmole^{-1} K
Absolute zero, 0°K = -273 C = 460 F
Volume of 1 k mole (STP) = 22.4 m^3 kmole
Mechanical equivalent of heat = 4185 J kcal^{-1}

D. Light

Vacuum speed of light = 2.9979×10^8 m/s
Ångstrom unit = 10^{-10} m

E. Electrical

Coulomb law constant = 9.00×10^9 N m^2 C^2
Permittivity of free space, $\varepsilon_o = 8.85 \times 10^{-12}$ F m^{-1}
Permeability of free space, $m_o = 4\pi \times 10^{-7}$ H m^{-1}
Faraday = 9.65×10^4 C m^{-1}

F. Atomic and nuclear physics

Rest mass of the electron, $m_e = 9.1091 \times 10^{-31}$ kg = 0.511 MeV
Electron charge, $e = 1.6021 \times 10^{-19}$ C
Specific charge of electron, $e/m = 1.7588 \times 10^{11}$ C/kg
Planck's constant, $h = 6.6257 \times 10^{-34}$ J sec = 4.136×10^{-15}eV s
Unified atomic mass unit (a.m.u.) = 1.661×10^{-27} kg = 931 MeV
1 curie = 3.700×10^{10} disintegrations/s
1 Angstrom unit = 10^{-10} meter = 10^5 Fermi
1 Fermi = 10^{-15} meter

2. Density of common substances (in gm per c.c.)

Solids	*Density*	*Liquids*	*Density*	*Gases (at NTP)*	*Density*
Aluminium	2.70	Alcohol (ethyl)	0.792	Air	0.001293
Brass	8.4-8.7	Glycerine	1.26	Carbon dioxide	0.00191977
Copper	8.93	Kerosene oil	0.799	Helium	0.0001785
Cork	0.22-0.26	Mercury	13.6	Hydrogen	0.0000899
Gold	19-32	Spirit	0.83	Nitrogen	0.001251
Glass (crown)	2.5-2.7	Milk	1.03	Oxygen	0.001429
Glass (Flint)	2.9-4.5	Olive oil	0.91-0.93	Steam (at 100°C)	0.000581
Glass (Pyrex)	2.25	Turpentine oil	0.87		
Iron (Cast)	7.1-7.7				
Iron (Wrought)	7.8-7.9				
Lead	11.37				
Paraffin wax	0.87-1.93				
Sodium chloride	2.17				
Sand (silver)	2.63				
Silver	10.5				
Steel	7.7-7.9				
Sugar	1.59				

3. Specific resistance and temperature coefficient of some solids

Material	*Specific resistance (x 10^8 ohm-m)*	*Temperature coefficient of resistance (x 10^{-4} °C^{-1})*	*Material*	*Specific resistance (x 10^8 ohm-m)*	*Temperature coefficient of resistance (x 10^{-4} °C^{-1})*
Aluminium	3.21	36	Nickel	11.8	27
Brass	6-9	10	Nichrome	110	1.7
Carbon lamp filament	4000	...	Platinum	11	37
Constantan	49	-0.4 to 0.1	Silver	1.63	40
Copper	1.78	42.8	Steel	19.9	16 to 42
German silver	16-40	2.3 to 6	Tin	11.3	45
Iron	1.3	62	Tungsten	5.5	51
Manganian	44.5	0.02 to 0.5	Zinc	6.1	37

4. E.M.F. of cells

Cell	*E.M.F. (Volts)*	*Cell*	*E.M.F. (Volts)*
Daniel	1.08-1.09	Cadmium at 20 °C	1.01854
Leclanche	1.45	Lead accumulator	1.9-2.2
Clark at 15 °C	1.433	Edison cell	1.45

Trigonometric Tables

Angle	Sin	Cos	Tan	Csc	Angle	Sin	Cos	Tan	Csc
1	0.017	1.000	0.017	57.299	46	0.719	0.695	1.036	1.390
2	0.035	0.999	0.035	28.654	47	0.731	0.682	1.072	1.367
3	0.052	0.999	0.052	19.107	48	0.743	0.669	1.111	1.346
4	0.070	0.998	0.070	14.336	49	0.755	0.656	1.150	1.325
5	0.087	0.996	0.087	11.474	50	0.766	0.643	1.192	1.305
6	0.105	0.995	0.105	9.567	51	0.777	0.629	1.235	1.287
7	0.122	0.993	0.123	8.206	52	0.788	0.616	1.280	1.269
8	0.139	0.990	0.141	7.185	53	0.799	0.602	1.327	1.252
9	0.156	0.988	0.158	6.392	54	0.809	0.588	1.376	1.236
10	0.174	0.985	0.176	5.759	55	0.819	0.574	1.428	1.221
11	0.191	0.982	0.194	5.241	56	0.829	0.559	1.483	1.206
12	0.208	0.978	0.213	4.810	57	0.839	0.545	1.540	1.192
13	0.225	0.974	0.231	4.445	58	0.848	0.530	1.600	1.179
14	0.242	0.970	0.249	4.134	59	0.857	0.515	1.664	1.167
15	0.259	0.966	0.268	3.864	60	0.866	0.500	1.732	1.155
16	0.276	0.961	0.287	3.628	61	0.875	0.485	1.804	1.143
17	0.292	0.956	0.306	3.420	62	0.883	0.469	1.881	1.133
18	0.309	0.951	0.325	3.236	63	0.891	0.454	1.963	1.122
19	0.326	0.946	0.344	3.072	64	0.899	0.438	2.050	1.113
20	0.342	0.940	0.364	2.924	65	0.906	0.423	2.145	1.103
21	0.358	0.934	0.384	2.790	66	0.914	0.407	2.246	1.095
22	0.375	0.927	0.404	2.669	67	0.921	0.391	2.356	1.086
23	0.391	0.921	0.424	2.559	68	0.927	0.375	2.475	1.079
24	0.407	0.914	0.445	2.459	69	0.934	0.358	2.605	1.071
25	0.423	0.906	0.466	2.366	70	0.940	0.342	2.747	1.064
26	0.438	0.899	0.488	2.281	71	0.946	0.326	2.904	1.058
27	0.454	0.891	0.510	2.203	72	0.951	0.309	3.078	1.051
28	0.469	0.883	0.532	2.130	73	0.956	0.292	3.271	1.046
29	0.485	0.875	0.554	2.063	74	0.961	0.276	3.487	1.040
30	0.500	0.866	0.577	2.000	75	0.966	0.259	3.732	1.035
31	0.515	0.857	0.601	1.942	76	0.970	0.242	4.011	1.031
32	0.530	0.848	0.625	1.887	77	0.974	0.225	4.331	1.026
33	0.545	0.839	0.649	1.836	78	0.978	0.208	4.705	1.022
34	0.559	0.829	0.675	1.788	79	0.982	0.191	5.145	1.019
35	0.574	0.819	0.700	1.743	80	0.985	0.174	5.671	1.015
36	0.588	0.809	0.727	1.701	81	0.988	0.156	6.314	1.012
37	0.602	0.799	0.754	1.662	82	0.990	0.139	7.115	1.010
38	0.616	0.788	0.781	1.624	83	0.993	0.122	8.144	1.008
39	0.629	0.777	0.810	1.589	84	0.995	0.105	9.514	1.006
40	0.643	0.766	0.839	1.556	85	0.996	0.087	11.430	1.004
41	0.656	0.755	0.869	1.524	86	0.998	0.070	14.301	1.002
42	0.669	0.743	0.900	1.494	87	0.999	0.052	19.081	1.001
43	0.682	0.731	0.933	1.466	88	0.999	0.035	28.636	1.001
44	0.695	0.719	0.966	1.440	89	1.000	0.017	57.290	1.000
45	0.707	0.707	1.000	1.414	90	1.000	0.000		1.000

5. Wavelength of emission of some standard sources

Source	*Wavelength (Å)*	*Source*	*Wavelength (Å)*
Mercury discharge	6232 orange 6152 orange 5791 yellow 5770 yellow 5461 green (bright, yellowish) 4960 green (faint) 4916 blue-green (faint) 4358 blue 4078 violet 4047 violet	Hydrogen discharge	6563 red 4861 blue-green 4340 blue 4102 blue 3970 violet 3889 violet
		Argon discharge	4628 4596 4511 4345 4334 4300 4272 4266 4259 4201 4198 4191 4182 4164 4159
Neon discharge	6929 6599 6507 6402 6383 6334 6217 6164 6143 6074 6030 5882 5852 5401 5341		
Sodium flame or discharge	5890 yellow (D_2 line) 5896 yellow		

6. Refractive indices of some solids for the mean D line of sodium 589.3 nm

Substance: Solids	*Refractive index*	*Substance: Liquids*	*Refractive index*
Glass crown	1.48-1.61	Alcohol ethyl	1.362
Glass flint	1.53-1.96	Alcohol methyl	1.329
Ice	1.31	Aniline	1.59
Mica	1.56-1.60	Benzene	1.504
Sugar	1.56	Glycerine	1.47
		Paraffin oil	1.44
		Turpentine	1.47
		Water	1.333

7. Dispersive power of some materials

Medium	*Dispersive power*	*Medium*	*Dispersive power*
Alcohol	0.0165	Flint glass	0.0271
Benzene	0.0338	Dense flint glass	0.2961
Crown glass	0.0193	Water	0.0180

8. Specific rotation of some substances

Active substance	*Solvent*	*Specific rotation at 20oC for sodium light 589.3 nm degree dm^{-1} $(gm/cc)^{-1}$*
Glucose	Water (20% solution)	+52.2
Cane sugar	Water (20% solution)	+66.5
Fructose	Water (20 % solution)	-37.0
Turpentine	Pure	-62.0
Nicotine	Pure	-91.5

9. Horizontal component of earth's magnetic field at different cities

City	*Angle of declination*	*Angle of dip*	*Horizontal component B_H (Orested)*
Agra	0°10'E	40°-40'	0.348
Ajmer	....	39°-46'	0.358
Aligarh	0°20'E	41°-50'	0.356
Allahabad	0°20'W	37°-10'	0.353
Bareily	0°20'E	42°20'	0.344
Bangalore	....	9°-21.2'	0.405
Bombay	0°20'W	25°-30'	0.376
Calcutta	0°00'	31°-30'	0.382
Dehradun	0°50'E	45°-50'	0.332
Delhi	0°40'E	42°52'	0.345
Hyderabad	....	19°-39.2'	0.397
Gorakhpur	0°20'W	39°-40'	0.358
Gwalior	0°20'E	39°-60'	0.353
Jaipur	0°30'E	40°-30'	0.347
Kanpur	0°00'	38°-39'	0.363
Lucknow	0°10'W	40°-00'	0.354
Ludhiana	....	45°-13.3'	0.335
Meerut	0°40'E	43°-30'	0.339
Varanasi	0°30'W	37°-10'	0.364

10. Band gap of some materials

Material	*Band gap at 300 K (eV)*	*Material*	*Band gap at 300 K (eV)*
Silicon	1.11	Indium (III) nitride	0.7
Selenium	1.74	Indium (III) phosphide	1.35
Germanium	0.67	Indium (III) arsenide)	0.36
Silicon carbide	2.86	Zinc oxide	3.37
Aluminium phosphide	2.45	Zinc sulphide	3.6
Aluminium arsenide	2.16	Zinc selenide	2.7
Aluminium antimonide	1.6	Zinc telluride	2.25
Aluminium nitrite	6.3	Cadmium sulphide	2.42
Diamond	5.5	Cadmium salenide	1.73
Gallium (III) phosphide	2.26	Cadmium telluride	1.49
Gallium (III) arsenide	1.43	Lead (II) sulfide	0.37
Gallium (III) nitride	3.4	Lead (II) selenide	0.27
Gallium (II) sulfide	2.5	Lead (II) telluride	0.29
Gallium antimonide	0.7	Copper (II) oxide	1.2